Learning in the Early Years

Knowledge & Understanding of the World

Helen Banks and Suzanne Handsley

Activities based on the Desirable Outcomes for under-fives

Ideas for planning, assessment and record-keeping

Photocop... ...rhymes and songs

Authors
Helen Banks and Suzanne Handsley

Series consultant
Pauline Kenyon

Editor
Sally Gray

Assistant editor
Lesley Sudlow

Series designer
Joy White

Designer
Rachel Warner

Illustrations
Peter Stevenson

Cover and photographs
Garry Clarke

The authors would like to acknowledge the support they received from Maddie with her ideas, questions and secretarial skills.

Designed using Adobe Pagemaker
Processed by Scholastic Ltd, Leamington Spa

Published by Scholastic Ltd, Villiers House, Clarendon Avenue,
Leamington Spa, Warwickshire CV32 5PR

With thanks to Military Road Lower School in Northampton and Rainbows End Nursery in Leamington Spa for allowing us to photograph their work with the children.

The publishers gratefully acknowledge permission to reproduce the following copyright material:
A. and C. Black with Inter-Action Inprint for 'I've Got A Body' by Harriet Powell from *Game Songs With Prof. Dogg's Troupe* © Harriet Powell (A. & C. Black and Inter-Action Inprint). **John Foster** for 'Weather bear' by John Foster © 1998 John Foster, previously unpublished. **Jillian Harker** for 'A Visit To The Park' and 'A Present For Granny' © 1998 Jillian Harker, previously unpublished. **Her Majesty's Stationery Office** for the use of text from the Department of Education and Employment/SCAA document *Nursery Education Desirable Outcomes for Children's Learning* © 1996, Crown copyright. **Jan Holdstock** for 'Birthday Song' from *Every Colour Under The Sun* by Jan Holdstock © 1983 Jan Holdstock (1983, Ward Lock Educational). **Johanne Levy** for the musical arrangement for 'The Wheels On The Bus' and 'Five Currant Buns' © 1998 Johanne Levy, previously unpublished. **Scholastic Ltd** for the use of 'Laura' by Michael Rosen from *The Hypnotiser* by Michael Rosen © 1988, Michael Rosen (1988, Andre Deutsch, an imprint of Scholastic Ltd). **The Watts Group** for 'Something Special' by Nicola Moon © 1995 Nicola Moon (1995, Orchard Books). Every effort has been made to trace copyright holders and the publishers apologise for any inadvertent omissions.

British Library Cataloguing-in-Publication Data
A catalogue record for this book is available from the British Library.

ISBN 0-590-53759-8

Contents

Introduction

A characteristic of young children is their constant need to explore the world around them. They go through stages of putting everything in their mouth or repeatedly dropping things out of the carrycot to see what happens. This is all a part of their search for pattern and order in the world.

As children grow older and their experience widens, the more they are able to make sense of the world and develop understandings based on similarities, differences, patterns and change. These are the processes that underpin the Area of Learning called Knowledge and Understanding of the World in the document *Desirable Outcomes for Children's Learning* published by the School Curriculum and Assessment Authority.

The Desirable Outcomes

Knowledge and Understanding of the World is probably the most all encompassing of the six Areas of Learning which is truly integrated and reflects the real way that young children learn. By exploring their environment and the world around them children will develop ideas that will form the basis of future learning in history, geography, science, design and technology and IT. Technology is part of the everyday lives of young children and they readily adapt to changes in it. It is important that they develop a confident approach to using a range of technology.

The Desirable Outcomes for this Area state that:

* *Children talk about where they live, their environment, their families and past and present events in their own lives.*

* *They show an awareness of the purposes of some features of the area in which they live.*

* *They explore and recognise features of living things, objects and events in the natural and made world and look closely at similarities, differences, patterns and change.*

*   *They talk about their observations, sometimes recording them and ask questions to gain information about why things happen and how things work.*
*   *They explore and select materials and equipment and use skills such as cutting, joining, folding and building for a variety of purposes.*
*   *They use technology, where appropriate, to support their learning.*

Throughout this book the Desirable Outcomes referred to are those published by the School Curriculum and Assessment Authority in *Desirable Outcomes for Children's Learning* for use in England. The ideas in this book can be applied equally well to the guidance documents on pre-school education published for Wales, Scotland and Northern Ireland.

The range of learning covered in Knowledge and Understanding of the World can seem daunting at first glance. However, the activities in this book show that all the aspects of learning can easily be developed through familiar play contexts and through the child's own home and local environment.

Delivering the curriculum

What resources will I need?

You do not necessarily require specialised or expensive resources. However, it is important that you know what you want children to learn from different activities, in order to make the most of opportunities provided.

Many of the activities that you might plan for themes such as 'Our homes', 'Pets' or 'Growing' relate to Knowledge and Understanding of the World. Plan for children to go on visits to other places or for walks in the local area. Such outings provide a wealth of opportunities for them to ask questions about how things work and why they happen and to talk about aspects of the local environment. Books, stories, videos and television programmes also provide a basis for extending children's understanding about the world around them.

Planning

What experiences do the children need?

It is important to remember that the Desirable Outcomes are *outcomes* for children aged five, they do not define the range of experiences that children should have. Try to ensure that children have opportunities to:

*   talk about where they live, their family and other people that they know, as well as events in their lives both past and present;
*   explore and observe their local environment and living things (themselves, plants and animals), talking and asking questions about what they see;
*   experiment with natural and manufactured objects, investigate and talk about similarities and differences, patterns and changes in living things, materials and the environment;
*   use a range of resources, materials and tools to make things for a variety of purposes, asking questions about why things happen and how they work;
*   develop the skills of cutting, joining, folding and building;
*   use technology such as a computer, tape-recorders and electronic toys;
*   talk about what they have done, and occasionally record their observations in pictorial form.

Planning ahead

It is important to plan ahead to ensure that these experiences are available to all the children. See Chapter 1, 'Planning' for more information. Your themes over the year need to be carefully planned in order to achieve a balance in this Area of Learning. For example 'Pets' would provide opportunities to look at living things whereas 'Toys' would provide a good focus for looking at what things are made from and how they work. In this way ideas for developing Knowledge and Understanding of the World can be built into an integrated curriculum.

Equal opportunities

Carefully monitor how children use the different areas of your setting to ensure that all children have equal access to the full range of experiences required. Make sure that boys do not dominate areas such as construction play or exploring new materials. It is important to ensure that both boys and girls are involved in these investigations so that positive attitudes to science and technology are developed for both genders at an early age.

It may be necessary to adapt some of the activities for children with special educational needs. However, it is important to ensure that all children have an equal chance to gain maximum access to the immediate and wider environment.

The integrated curriculum

The range of skills, knowledge and understanding included in this Area of Learning can be developed when children are engaging in the usual activities in your setting, as well as when you plan specific activities to develop their Knowledge and Understanding of the World,

Sand and water play provide opportunities to experiment with materials, exploring how and why things work. Construction toys and blocks allow children to build and design for a variety of purposes and require them to explore and select materials and equipment. In role-play, and in using small world play items such as a model house, garage or hospital, the children naturally talk about themselves and their families. Stories and rhymes provide ideal stimuli for children to talk about events in their own lives and help them to develop a sense of the passage of time. In addition, the outdoor area has great potential for exploring the immediate environment. The local community is another important learning source – take the children out to look closely at the streets, houses, shops and any interesting features of the local environment.

Safety

Young children need constant and careful supervision. Be vigilant and try to anticipate hazards – if sand or water is spilled, clean it up immediately; do not allow a child to build a model in an unsafe place, such as behind the door and always keep the room tidy and clean.

Ensure that the materials the children work with are suitable for the age range. Supervise the children closely when they are working with small or sharp objects and keep them well away from heat sources during cookery activities. When taking the children on an outing check the Local Authority regulations for the correct adult to child ratio. Send a letter home to parents/carers asking for their permission to take their child on outings. Make sure that you are aware of any allergies, illnesses or other health considerations concerning the children.

Assessment and record-keeping

Detailed guidance on assessment and record-keeping is given in Chapter 3. Keeping careful records of assessments is an important part of your curriculum planning and you will find helpful photocopiable assessment and record-keeping sheets on pages 73-75. These show the development of children's early skills and knowledge in history, geography, science and technology.

Working with parents

Parents are a wonderful source of information for this Area of Learning and it is important that they are made to feel part of your group. They may be able to provide stories, photographs or local knowledge to support your investigations of the locality or for looking at families. An ideal opportunity to enlist the support of parents is when taking a trip into your local community. The better the adult/child ratio, the more the children will gain from the experience. Involving parents also provides an opportunity to explain the learning that the children are developing.

How to use this book

This book is organised into separate sections to help you plan and deliver a broad and balanced curriculum for Knowledge and Understanding of the World:
* Chapter 1 'Planning' suggests how to focus your planning in the short-, medium- and long-term.
* Chapter 2 'Child development' explains the ways in which young children start to acquire early skills and concepts.
* Chapter 3 'Assessment and record-keeping' explains how to plan and carry out assessments and how to share information about children's learning with parents and carers.
  The main bulk of the book concentrates on practical activity chapters:
* Chapter 4 'Myself and others' builds on children's experiences in their family and provides a framework for sequencing events in time.
* Chapter 5 'Living things' explores the features of plants and animals.
* Chapter 6 'Exploring our environment' helps children to become more aware of sights and sounds around them and the purpose of places in their locality.
* Chapter 7 'Objects and materials' develops scientific understanding.
* Chapter 8 'How things work' focuses on design and technology skills.
  At the end of the activity chapters you will find a photocopiable section including assessment and recording sheets, rhymes, stories and songs to accompany some of the activities, and activity sheets for the children. The final page is a list of recommended resources to accompany this Area of Learning.

Other books in the series

The same format is used for the other five books in the series, which each cover one of the Areas of Learning: *Language and Literacy, Mathematics, Personal and Social Development, Physical Development* and *Creative Development*.
  A seventh book *Ready for Inspection* covers all the management issues you will need to consider to prepare for a successful inspection.

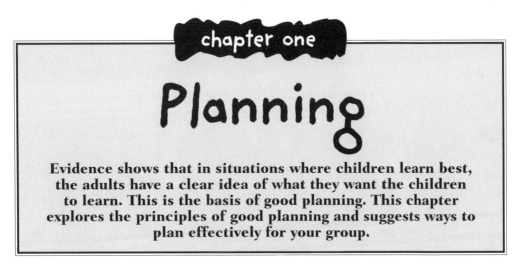

chapter one

Planning

Evidence shows that in situations where children learn best, the adults have a clear idea of what they want the children to learn. This is the basis of good planning. This chapter explores the principles of good planning and suggests ways to plan effectively for your group.

Why plan?

When working with young children it is important to decide together as a staff what knowledge, skills and attitudes you would like the children to develop and then design activities and experiences that will help them to achieve these. For example, if you want children to develop joining skills it is important that you provide plenty of opportunities for them to use different types of glue, Sellotape, staplers, paper fasteners and so on. Young children need experience over time and in a range of contexts before they can confidently use and apply their new knowledge and understanding. It is therefore necessary to provide a range of experiences over time to develop and reinforce specific learning objectives or intentions.

A flexible approach

When working with young children it is vital that approaches to planning are flexible. It is not helpful if children are forced to complete certain activities. Effective learning is more likely to take place if children are interested and readily engage in the provided activities. They may not wish to play a specific game on Monday, but if learning opportunities are planned over a period of time they may be ready to play the game at another time.

It is also important to respond to children's interests as they arise. If you have a clear understanding about the range of learning intentions you want children to develop, you are much better prepared to respond constructively to the children's

natural curiosity and enthusiasm. For example, if the children find some snails in the outside area while they are playing and you have planned to cover some work on the features of living things, then use this opportunity to talk about how the snail moves, to look at how it protects itself and to discuss what it might eat. In this way planning should always support learning.

Similarly, if you have planned to read a particular story to the children and a child comes in with a new book, is full of enthusiasm and wants to share it with their friends, then it would be inappropriate for you to stick rigidly to your plans. However, if you do make significant changes to your plans, you may need to include the original plans in the next part of your programme.

Keeping the evidence

It is important to keep evidence of your planning for a variety of reasons. Not least because it will help you with your planning in the future. Plans for specific activities or learning intentions within each of the Areas of Learning could be collated in a file for use at an appropriate time in the next year. This process should also help to reduce repetition in paperwork and leave you the time and energy to focus on how the children are learning.

A file or 'scheme of work' including activities to develop learning in children's Knowledge and Understanding of the World is a valuable resource to build up over time.

Once you have collected a range of activities it would be helpful to order these by their level of difficulty in terms of the knowledge, skills and concepts that are involved. In this way you will have the support you need to plan for progression and to match activities to children's abilities and needs.

Preparing for inspection

It is important to retain your plans to provide evidence of your work in preparation for inspections of your setting. The content of the educational programme and the planning form a significant part of what the inspectors use to form their judgements about the quality of your provision. Your plans should provide vital evidence for how you ensure that children obtain a balanced curriculum within Knowledge and Understanding of the World.

When reviewing your plans the inspectors will be looking for evidence that children are given opportunities to explore their local environment, perhaps using photographs, talking to visitors or going on exploratory walks round the area. This may also include visits to local shops or the park. As these are unlikely to take place during an inspection, your plans will provide evidence, not only of the trips and events, but also show what it is that you wanted the children to learn and your evaluation of how well the activity went.

The inspectors will want to know what opportunities the children have to talk about where they live, their families and past events in their lives. Once again, photographs can provide evidence of your planning.

Inspectors will also want to know what opportunities and resources are planned to encourage children to investigate and ask questions about how things work and to make things and use a variety of tools and equipment. Plans which indicate how you encourage children to record their observations and ideas in various ways will also be helpful, especially if they are backed up with samples of the children's work.

Using resources

Children are required to have access to technological resources but many settings will not have permanent access to a computer, nor is this necessary. In your planning you will be able to show how you arrange for children to use resources such as a tape-recorder, telephone, electronic toys, calculators and if possible a computer. Often these will be borrowed, or on loan for a limited period, and your planning may be the only evidence of their use.

In the area of Knowledge and Understanding of the World it is particularly important that you plan carefully how you want the children to work with the resources provided. It is not sufficient to simply provide the resources, rather it is important to focus on the processes of investigating similarities and differences, and talking about how and why things work. Over time you will notice the difference in the way that the children approach the activities.

The planning cycle

In order to ensure that all children have access to a broad and balanced range of activities, planning needs to be broken down into several stages – long-term, medium-term and short-term.

Long-term planning

Long-term planning for Knowledge and Understanding of the World should indicate what opportunities occur for children to develop an understanding of how and why things happen, to use building skills and so on. The plans should show how different areas of your setting will be utilised in the activities provided. In order to plan for this some practitioners take one area at a time such as sand or construction toys and record how these can be used to develop the various aspects of Knowledge and Understanding of the World. If only some activities are available for each session, or if access to some resources occurs only at certain times in the year, such as the water play being outdoors in the summer, a timetable illustrating the availability of these resources should be included.

Long-term planning should also indicate how the topics or themes that have been chosen for the year (or a longer period if a rolling programme is in place), relate to different aspects of Knowledge and Understanding of the World. For example, a topic on the farm will provide plenty of opportunities to talk about the features of living things, and a topic on the weather would be a good focus for looking at similarities and differences, patterns and change. You should check that the topics you have chosen provide a balanced experience across all the aspects of Knowledge and Understanding of the World, as well as the five other Areas of Learning.

Knowledge and Understanding of the World		LONG-TERM PLANNING
	Topics/Focus	Key skills/Areas of Learning
A U T U M N	Toys (9 weeks) • Making puppets • Wheels and moving parts • Old and new toys • Different materials • Computer use • Clothes for toys • Special toys	Talk about different toys, materials, types, favourites. Technology skills – cutting and joining, simple puppet toys. Looking at different toys – how they move, how old are they, who owns them. Making toys with moving parts (junk modelling). Dressing dolls and teddies for different weather – similarities and differences in materials. Computer – 'Dressing Teddy'.
	Christmas (2 weeks)	Technology – making cards, wrapping paper, decorations. Talking about Christmas in the past – own and Christmas story.
S P R I N G	All around us (5 weeks) • Visit to the park • Visit to shops • Planting seeds for garden • Plants	Talk about environment – what they like/don't like. Make own environment in the sand etc. Watch seeds grow – talk about what the seeds need. Look at other plants and pictures of living things.
	Our weather (4 weeks) • Night and day • Patterns around us	Observe changes in the weather – record weather in pictures. Talk about the differences between night and day. Look for patterns in the environment – on walls, in clouds, on clothes, posters etc.
S U M M E R	On the farm (6 weeks) • Farm animals • Farm visit • Food from farms • Pets • Working animals	Visit farm – talk about living/non-living things. Record 'special event' in photos. Different types of farm (arable, dairy, hill, fish). Group animals into different types – wild animals, pet animals, farm animals – what do the animals eat?
	The seaside (6 weeks) • Seasons • Sunshine • Seaside visit • Life in/under the sea	Seasons and weather in summer. Record special events in the year in photos – make book with children's memories. Sun and shadows. Safety in the sun. Holidays. Explore beach environment on trip – what lives in the rock pools? Who is the café for? Set up the role-play area as a beach café. Summer clothes. Travelling to the sea (simple maps, different transport).

Medium-term planning

In medium-term planning you need to identify learning opportunities for shorter blocks of time, such as a period of two to three weeks or half a term. These plans may be based on a particular topic or theme such as 'Toys' or 'My family'.

The medium-term plans need to identify clearly what aspects of Knowledge and Understanding of the World you wish the children to learn and how these are developed by the activities that you plan. For example, your learning objective may be to encourage children to ask questions about how things work and in order to achieve this you plan to put out all the wheeled toys for outdoor play.

The format of the activities in this book supports this stage of planning. By collating planning at this stage it is also possible to build up a bank of activities or a 'scheme of work' for Knowledge and Understanding of the World. Opportunities for assessment should also be identified and logged at this stage of planning. This aspect is developed further in Chapter 3, 'Assessment and record-keeping'.

Knowledge and Understanding of the World	Topic: Toys	Autumn term (9 weeks)	MEDIUM-TERM PLANNING
Learning objectives	Activities
Week 1 • Find out about materials used to make toys. • Talk about similarities and differences in materials.	Make a collection of children's toys. Talk about which ones are made from the same material – wood, plastic, metal etc. Talk about which materials are hard, soft, strong, bendy and so on.
Week 2 • Investigate how different toys move. • Use the words push, pull, turn etc.	Select toys that can be moved, and wheeled vehicles in nursery. Ask questions about how they move. Introduce the appropriate words to describe how they move. Look at clockwork, battery power, friction drive and remote-controlled toys.
Week 3 • Talk about when and from where they got their toys. • Look at the differences and similarities between old and new toys.	Children each bring in a special toy. Talk about when they got it – Was it a birthday/Christmas present? Did they go to the shops to get it? Paint picture of toy and record the children's comments about when they got it. Look at old and new toys – differences, similarities and change.

Short-term planning

Short-term plans will be more focused on what happens on a weekly or daily basis. Well-structured long- and medium-term planning should help to support short-term planning. Short-term plans need to show who is doing what and when. They are likely to be based on daily routines and need to show when specific resources are required or when particular events are to take place. They should be the focus for a dialogue between the adults involved in the setting, including voluntary helpers. In this way all the adults in a setting should be clear about what they are expected to do.

The short-term plans should also indicate if certain activities are to be used for assessment purposes and how, such as using a collection of babies' clothes for the children to demonstrate what they know about different materials. It is important that short-term plans reflect your ongoing assessment of children's needs. For example, if in the previous week, staff noticed that several children were experiencing difficulty using glue then the following week's plans should include adult support to help those children use glue effectively.

Short-term plans will also focus more specifically on the needs of individual children or groups of children. Systematic planning of this kind will also help you to focus on what learning is significant and to collect information for your record-keeping on individual children. The short-term plans should be working documents and staff often develop their own forms of shorthand to communicate with each other. It would clearly be unwieldy to write everything down, and the ongoing dialogue between staff with regard to what children are doing and learning is an important part of short-term planning. The essential ingredient of good planning is that you are focused on the learning potential of different situations.

SHORT-TERM PLANNING				Autumn term (Week 9) Christmas			
Mon	Personal & Social	Language & Literacy	Maths	Knowledge & Understanding	Creative Development	Physical Development	Comments
9.00	Home Groups News Weather (cold) attributes and weather board (chart and signs)	Discussing change and listening to each other	Sorting the weather symbols and date	Talking about different weather			
9.20			Home groups Counting rhymes '5 speckled frogs' Counting days to Christmas (number line)				
	(Tim – Green & Red groups)			(Blue & Yellow groups – Lyn & Julie leading session)			
9.30–10.00	Role-play Preparing for a party (dressing-up clothes, play food, mats, beakers, decorations)	Book corner, making 'Happy Christmas' cards (card templates, foil, glue, scissors, felt-tipped pens)		Christmas story (Look at maps of Holy Land and Christian artefacts)	Making Christmas decorations and lanterns (foil, paper, glue, scissors, felt-tipped pens)	Cutting and sticking skills (Lyn – Blue & Yellow groups) Outdoor activities	Julie leads in story and making decorations
10.00				(Green & Red groups – Tim & Julie) Christmas story (as	(as above)	Roadways (cones) and traffic lights, cars and	Julie will demonstrate making decorations
10.30	Home Groups Snack time (milk and biscuits) review of activities			above)		trailers	

Teamwork and support

These stages of planning may appear rather daunting to begin with, but it is important to remember that your plans will develop and become more consistent over time.

The process of planning is as important as the pieces of paper themselves. Make sure that you plan together as a staff, including all staff members, volunteers and students. Through careful collaborative planning, a group of staff will develop a better understanding of what is involved in Knowledge and Understanding of the World, as well as the other Areas of Learning. In this way you will be able to ensure adequate coverage of all aspects of the subject area and everyone will feel more confident in their own ability to support children's learning effectively. Staff working with young children often express a lack of knowledge about the principles underlying this Area of Learning, such as scientific processes and technology and its uses. In planning together staff should become clearer in their expectations of what and how children learn about the world around them.

Partnership with parents

The plans can also be a useful way of explaining to parents what range of experiences are included under the heading Knowledge and Understanding of the World. Display a flow chart for your current topic, showing how the activities are to be used to develop Knowledge and Understanding of the World. This will enable parents to encourage their children to talk about what they have been doing and to build on these experiences at home.

Parents can also be involved in the Area of Knowledge and Understanding of the World by contributing background information (such as baby photographs) which you may be collecting for work with the children.

Sharing plans with parents also creates further opportunities for developing a working partnership. You may find that your parents have hidden talents or hobbies such as an interesting collection of old toys which they would be willing to show to the children in connection with a relevant topic.

Mixed-age classes

In many schools, particularly small ones, staff have to teach mixed-age classes. Children under-five may be grouped with five-, six- and seven-year-olds and planning systems would have to take account of the wide range of needs of the children, as well as the requirements of Key Stage 1 and the Desirable Outcomes for Learning. Often it is possible to have the same focus for the different age groups but with differentiation by outcome or by task. For example, all the children could be involved in growing seeds – the youngest children could observe and talk about what happens to the seeds and the older ones could investigate the conditions that favour growth, writing about their findings.

The planning formats that you design would have to show what you plan for under-fives in terms of Knowledge and Understanding of the World, next to planning for science, design and technology, IT, history and geography for Key Stage 1. You need to ensure that the experiences planned for under-fives are activity-based and involve a reasonable amount of choice.

In long-term planning for mixed-age classes you will need to consider which aspects of science, geography and so on need to be covered by each age group and then ensure that your medium-term plans provide adequate coverage of these areas. You will need to include a wider range of topics over a longer period than is usual with single age groups in order to maintain the children's interest and to prevent repetition. The range of knowledge that is required for Knowledge and Understanding of the World and the related National Curriculum areas is likely to be a significant factor in determining the choice of topics. This is not an easy task and the role of planning is crucial in such cases for ensuring that all children receive appropriate coverage of the curriculum.

chapter two

Child development

The experience of babies is limited to what they can see, hear and touch within their immediate environment. As children become more mobile and their language skills develop, their ability to explore the world expands.

Starting with the child

We know that children learn best when they are actively involved and interested in what is happening around them. It is therefore important that you plan experiences for young children that are relevant to their world. They will only be able to relate to new experiences if these occur in contexts that make some sense to them. This is why young children have so much difficulty with abstract learning, because this is 'disembedded' from their experience of the world.

The more opportunities that children have for exploration, the more they are able to predict what is going to happen in certain situations, such as knowing that if they drop a rubber ball it will bounce. This way they are able to become more confident in their knowledge about the world. Children also feel actively involved if the activity is directly related to their own experience, which many of the activities in this book aim to be, such as 'Do you remember when?' and 'Last week, this week, next week' in Chapter 4. Photographs also hold a great fascination for young children. These provide ideal opportunities to extend children's understanding of their place within their family and the order of events in time.

Extending learning

Initially children's knowledge of the world is closely tied to experiences within their own home and family. It is through contact with other children and adults in settings such as playgroups, nurseries and schools that they begin to compare their own experiences with those of others. In so doing they broaden their concepts of the world and their place within it.

15

Much of children's early play can be seen as a way of exploring different roles and situations and this is well supported by opportunities to use different role-play contexts, small world play, puppets and a range of imaginative play. In so doing children also come into contact with, and begin to develop an understanding of, their own and other cultures. It is therefore important to ensure that the play opportunities and resources that you provide support cultural diversity and equal opportunities.

Visits to different places of interest within their local community help children to learn about the different roles that people fulfil. The park, the shops and the local health centre are all places of relevance to the children's own interests, and at the same time they offer experiences which extend their knowledge about what people do and how they behave in different settings. It is important to structure these visits and build them into your planning. Help children to make sense of these experiences for themselves through role-play after the visit, such as in the activity 'The health centre' in Chapter 6.

Active learning is important

As well as being actively involved, young children also learn best through actions rather than through instruction. From an early age, infants pursue this desire to act on the world. They drop objects over the side of their pram to see what will happen and, once they are able to move, try to touch objects or put them in their mouths. This willingness to explore the world around them forms the origins of a developing scientific awareness. It is usually accompanied by a sense of excitement and fun. This is something that needs to be nurtured when providing educational experiences for young children.

The role of language

Children's reasoning often appears very different to that of adults. This is because they only have a partial understanding of a situation, and do not yet have the necessary experience to develop a more complete picture. In order to make sense of children's responses, and have some idea of what new experiences would help to develop their understanding further, try and understand how they are making sense within their own knowledge about the world – their own 'frame of reference'. When children are very young we can only surmise this from their actions. For example, studies of babies have shown that they are responsive to changes in facial expression at an early age.

Once children learn to talk, language becomes a powerful vehicle for sharing and developing their understanding of the world. It is therefore very important to establish a dialogue with children when they are involved in activities, in order to gain some insight into how they are interpreting what is happening and to give them the language that they need to describe their observations. This is why each activity in the book includes some suggestions for questions to ask the children.

Time to play

Play is the most important means by which young children learn. When children play they feel that they are in control of what is happening and are more confident to have a go, and therefore push their understanding to the limits. Close observation of children's play over a long period of time has revealed that there are often clear patterns in the way that they behave. For example, children may spend a lot of time covering things over – they will paint all over a piece of paper, make dens by covering chairs with a blanket and cover the floor with shapes. When this happens it can be difficult to distract them from their particular way of learning about the world. In this instance it is perhaps more appropriate to watch the way that they are behaving and adapt your activities to suit their approach. For example, if you were planning to do the activity 'Shoes' in Chapter 7, it might suit a child who is at the stage of covering things to suggest that they make a paper table cloth or a book cover by printing with shoe patterns.

The activities in this book should be used in a flexible way. With young children it will always be necessary to make adaptations to suit the way that they are learning.

Developing understanding

In order to find out how things work and to develop rudimentary scientific concepts, children need to actively experiment for themselves.

Children need experiences such as putting a range of objects and materials into water and observing what happens, before they begin to understand what is meant by floating and sinking. They need to actively use a range of vehicles and outdoor wheeled toys before they can develop an understanding of basic forces and the terms push, pull, twist and turn.

All the activities in Chapter 7, 'Objects and materials' involve actively experimenting with materials and objects, such as trying out different types of whisk or blowing different materials with a straw. These are specific opportunities planned in order that children can try out early scientific ideas. Many other opportunities are likely to arise through the children's play with other resources and through the questions that they raise. You need to be alert to opportunities that arise to foster their natural sense of enquiry and their need to make sense of the world.

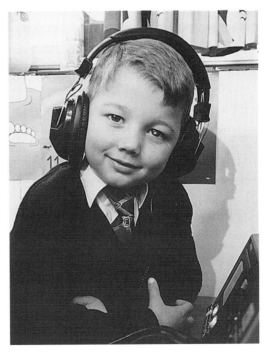

Many of the activities in Chapter 8 encourage the children to make products such as puppets, greetings cards or models. In developing the skills of cutting, folding, joining and building, and in using a range of technology, young children begin to establish some sense of control of the material world. All the activities in Chapter 8 focus on early technological understanding.

Establishing identity

Through a combination of language and action, children construct a network of understandings about the world. Their place within their family and within time is part of a complex network of relationships. The relationships that children make with significant people in their lives are of central importance to their development socially, emotionally and intellectually.

Children need to talk about their own families a great deal in order to establish a sense of their own identity and their role within the family. In comparing their experiences with those of their peers, they will begin to develop a concept of the relationships that can exist in families and how families change over time. These form the basis of a sense of history which will be extended as children are able to consider events before their own lifetime. The activities in Chapter 4, 'Myself and others' all focus on helping children to explore their role within the family and to realise how they themselves change as they grow older. Some of the activities such as 'Do you remember when?', further develop a sense of past and present in relation to the social group at the early years setting.

As children explore more of their own neighbourhood and further afield, they will also begin to develop their sense of place within the immediate environment. This is the beginning of geographical understanding. This is another reason why planned trips to significant places in the locality are valuable. If children have a chance to look at the range of shops that are available near to them they will be able to think about what these are used for and who uses them. In using playmats and making their own plans, children are developing early map work skills.

The activities in this book, therefore, support early understanding which will enhance later learning in science, technology, history and geography. The children themselves will not be aware of these distinctions, but it is important that the adults who plan their learning experiences have some understanding of how this learning develops.

chapter three

Assessment and record-keeping

Focused and systematic observation of young children's learning is an essential ingredient in good early years practice. This chapter provides valuable guidance for careful and systematic assessment and record-keeping procedures.

The importance of assessment

You need to know what children know already, what interests them and how they approach learning in order that you can plan activities that will take the children on to the next stage of learning. Many assessments are made on an informal day-to-day basis and it is important that you share these observations with colleagues, in order to build up a rounded picture of each child's stage of development.

A great deal of valuable information can be acquired this way but there will always be gaps in terms of Areas of Learning that have not been assessed. It is very important to identify specific opportunities for making assessments when planning activities. For example, it would be appropriate to use an opportunity when children make books about themselves and their families, to assess their ability to talk about their families. Knowledge and Understanding of the World is a broad subject area and it is vital to identify assessment opportunities to ensure adequate coverage of this Area of Learning.

Systematic assessment of children's skills, knowledge, understanding and attitudes should help you to build on children's prior learning. For example, if a child shows little interest in activities about using the senses, you will need to try and engage her in this type of activity (possibly by adapting the activity to suit her interests) before moving on to talking about or recording your observations.

Another purpose of assessment is to track children's development over time. Observations of children over a period of time will provide evidence of what they have learned in the setting. In other words this is a measure of the value added by the learning environment. Share these observations with parents to demonstrate what their children have learned.

National Baseline Assessment

As from September 1998, all schools in England and Wales will be required to undertake formalised 'Baseline Assessment' during the first half-term that the child is in a reception class. All Baseline Assessment systems from 1998 have to be accredited by the DfEE, with each child being assessed against criteria which show progression *towards* the Desirable Outcomes for Learning and Level 1 of the National Curriculum, in at least Language and Literacy and Mathematics. This information can then be used to evaluate children's progress at the end of Key Stage 1. Most systems of Baseline Assessment will also record children's development in the other Desirable Outcomes, including Knowledge and Understanding of the World. This provides valuable information that can be used to plan an appropriate curriculum for that group of learners. For example, if a group of children enter school demonstrating competence in using equipment and technology skills, then it will be necessary for staff to plan to provide more challenging design and technology tasks.

Assessments from pre-school settings can be considered as part of the Baseline Assessment, which should encourage schools and pre-school providers to work together. It is also expected that parents should be involved in discussions about Baseline Assessment. It makes sense, therefore, that your assessment procedures will be in line with these arrangements.

Linking planning and assessment

It is important that learning opportunities are planned carefully in order to give a balanced programme and to ensure that all aspects of Knowledge and Understanding of the World are covered over a period of time. For instance, does the programme give plenty of opportunities for children to explore the features of the natural and made world? Have you planned opportunities to explore the local environment? Are staff aware of the need to encourage children to look closely at similarities, differences, patterns and change in a variety of contexts and how do you plan to make sure that all children have these experiences?

When you produce your long-term plans to ensure balanced curriculum coverage over a year, it should be possible to identify topics which will provide opportunities for assessment of particular aspects of Knowledge and Understanding of the World. For example, a topic on 'the park' could provide an ideal opportunity to assess the children's ability to talk about some features of their area, or a topic on 'machines' would provide plenty of opportunities to assess design and technology skills. Identify these assessment opportunities at this stage using an asterisk in order to spread them out in a manageable way across the year.

Similarly, when you develop these topics in your medium-term plans, take note of the assessment opportunities asterisked and mark them again on your plans. This way you can check that your assessment goals are manageable and do not all occur at the same time. Make your own planned activities into assessment opportunities. For instance, when children are making cards and envelopes to use in the Christmas postbox, this would be a good time to assess their folding skills. Open-ended activities are better than tightly-prescribed activities. A child's own drawing about where they live will tell you much more about their understanding than colouring in features on a worksheet.

In your short-term plans you should identify how the assessments will be made in more detail. For instance, use an activity involving growing cress to assess children's understanding of the features of plants, and what plants need to grow by talking to each child as they observe the cress on a daily basis.

The assessment process

When to assess?

Ideally you will want to make an early assessment of each new child, after an appropriate settling-in period, to give you their stage of development on entry to your setting. It is likely that you would want to assess their personal and social skills and language abilities first, as these have a significant effect on all the other Areas of Learning. However, it is important to extend this initial assessment to all Areas of Learning, including Knowledge and Understanding of the World, in order that you are aware of what children know and can do as a starting point for planning new learning opportunities.

The photocopiable assessment and record-keeping sheets on pages 73–75 provide a format for doing this. There are three columns, one for each term in the pre-school setting. This should help you to chart each child's development over time. Your medium-term plans should help you to plan when these assessments will occur during the year.

Who assesses?

All those who have dealings with the children in the setting should be involved in their assessment, as everyone has useful observations to contribute. However, everyone should be very clear about what is being assessed, and the details of the assessment included in your short-term plans should ensure this common understanding. For example, providing a display of safe kitchen tools could be planned as an opportunity to assess the extent to which children ask questions about how things work. The person doing the assessment will need to listen to children's conversation while actively exploring the display in order to do this.

Assign a 'key-worker' for each group, whose responsibility it is to gather information from assessors and update records for all the children in their group.

It is also helpful to liaise with the next phase in the children's education to ensure that up-to-date records are passed on. These can then form part of the initial assessment in the next phase.

How can we assess?

Some assessments can be made by looking at an end product, such as a model that a child has made, but this leaves out vital information such as knowing what skills they were using to make the model. In making assessments it is usually necessary to observe the children involved in an activity and to listen to what they have to say. You will need to get alongside the child when they are playing. Establish a relationship in which the child feels confident and free to talk about what they are doing or observing. For example, when making biscuits ask specific questions such as: Are the biscuits the same as before we put them in the oven? This will encourage the children to observe and describe changes. The observer can then make notes on what the particular children did or said or tick pre-stated criteria.

Name __Sarah Caink_____

Knowledge and Understanding

Skills and concepts	Baseline/1st assessment Date
SCIENCE	
Can explore and recognise features of:	
* objects and events in the natural and made world;	Sorted the shells into groups – talked about their colours. 14/9
* living things.	Showed interest in watering the plants. 16/9
Looks closely at:	
* similarities;	Talked about the play dough going hard when left out. 3/10
* differences;	
* patterns;	
* change.	
Asks questions about:	
* why things happen;	Spent a long time using the wind up car – talked about the key making it go. 21/9
* how things work.	
Can:	
* talk about his/her observations;	Drew a picture of her own car moving. 21/9
* record his/her observations.	

Consider targeting children for observation on a rolling programme. For each session you could select two children to observe, focusing on an aspect of knowledge and understanding such as their ability to make observations. At the end of the session spend a few minutes pooling your observations with other staff members, with one person recording these in a file under the appropriate heading. Have pages for each child with headings for each Desirable Outcome. It will be particularly important to use assessment to identify and support children with special educational needs.

How can we record?

The above system and the assessment and record-keeping sheets are two ways of recording assessments. It is also useful to collect samples of children's work, such as drawings, photographs of models and so on to create an individual portfolio. Keep these in a folder for each child or mounted in a scrapbook. This is a good way of valuing children's achievements and sharing work with parents and carers. However, many aspects of children's development at this age are to do with active learning and may not result in an end product. It is therefore important to keep records of your observations of skills and understanding demonstrated in process.

Involving parents and carers

Try to establish good contacts with parents and carers before a child starts at your setting. This could be done by home-visiting or during the child's first visit to the setting. A range of information about the child can be collected on these occasions, including the parents' or carers' knowledge about the child's interests and abilities. The more that you know about the child's immediate and extended family and their home environment, the easier it will be for you to discuss these with the child and widen their understanding. These occasions also provide opportunities to give parents and carers information about the curriculum, including what Knowledge and Understanding of the World involves.

Arrange to discuss a child's progress with their parents or carers as soon after your first assessment as possible. Use this opportunity to explain how you use assessments to build on what the children already know and can do, and to suggest

one or two target areas that the parents can help to develop with their child at home. For example, you may ask a parent to encourage a child to bring in items from home, or some photographs, to provide opportunities to talk about the past and significant events in their lives.

It is also useful to send newsletters home which give an outline of the work the children will be covering in the coming weeks and the purpose of the activities. For example, you might say, 'We are making a collection of toys so that the children can find out what materials are used to make them'. Wherever possible include ideas for how parents can support their child's learning at home. Photographs and displays of work also provide an opportunity to show what the children have learned, particularly if you include children's comments about their learning.

chapter four

Myself and others

In this chapter the children are encouraged to explore their own individuality and how they relate to family and friends. They will be helped to notice similarities and differences between themselves and others.

The new baby

Learning outcome

To be aware of the needs of babies and how babies change as they grow.

Group size
Whole group.

What you need
Photos of staff and children as babies, a willing parent with their new baby.

Preparation
Make a display with the photos of children and staff when they were babies. Arrange for a parent to bring a new baby into a session. Ask her/him to bring a few articles of clothing and the main equipment necessary for looking after the baby. Explain to the parent how you expect the session to run and ask her/him to be prepared to talk about the new baby and answer the children's questions.

Discuss the forthcoming visit and help the children to explore what they already know about babies and to plan questions they could ask. Look at the photographs and talk about the changes that happen as people grow up.

What to do
Settle the children so that they can all see the parent and the baby. Invite your visitor to tell the children about the routine of the baby's day. Suggest that they show the clothing, toys and equipment that the baby needs. Ask him/her to bath, change or feed the baby if possible. Take photos of the baby, parent and sibling for follow-up discussion and display.

Encourage the children to ask questions or make comments throughout the session.

Finish by asking the children to sing a lullaby to the baby.

Questions to ask
What things can you do that the baby can't do yet? Can the baby eat the same food as you? How have you changed since you were a baby?

For younger children
Work with a small group of four to six children. Encourage younger children to play at parenting by caring for a doll. Give them opportunities to dress and undress the doll.

For older children
Write letters to thank the parent and baby for visiting. Talk about and record a sequence of events in a baby's day.

Follow-up activities
∗ Complete the worksheet on page 88. The children are asked to create a set of toys appropriate for babies and a set for themselves.
∗ Invite a Health Visitor or School Nurse to come in and talk about a baby clinic.
∗ Design a baby's toy.

Links with home

Ask parents to lend photos or videos of their child as a baby. Ask them to talk to their child about the things they did when they were a baby.

A book about me

Learning outcome

To develop awareness of each person's individuality.

Group size
Four to six children.

What you need

The story 'Something special' on pages 80–81, a selection of photos showing you, your family, pets and so on, something that is special to you, a favourite book, a special container to display books.

Work with small groups of children over a period of one to two weeks, completing one or two pages at each session. Encourage the children to illustrate their books with drawings, photographs and by sticking in pictures. Help them with their writing. As books are completed, display them in a special container so that the children can choose to read their own and each other's books.

Preparation

Make individual (A5) books using two sheets of A4 folded paper. Name the title page 'All About Me' with space for a drawing or photo. Label each page with a different heading such as 'My Favourite Toy'; 'My Family'; 'My Pets' and so on.

What to do

Read the story 'Something special' to the whole group. Explain to the children that they are each going to make a book about themselves. Show them the books you have prepared.

Show the children the photos and 'favourite things' you have brought in. Tell them why they are special to you. Encourage the children to talk about their families and their favourite things. What things don't they like? Suggest that the children bring in a couple of favourite things and photographs to show everyone. Make sure the children do not bring in anything too valuable and ensure that the things they bring in are clearly labelled to take home afterwards.

Questions to ask

What do you like to eat/drink best? Do you have a baby in your family? Which television programmes do you like best?

For younger children

Work with two to three children in a group. The book could be given to parents and children to complete and bring with them when they start school, nursery or playgroup.

For older children

Let older children offer suggestions of what to put in the book. Encourage them to use the book to begin a portfolio of their work that will go with them as they get older.

Follow-up activities

∗ Make a block graph of favourite foods.
∗ Make an alphabet of children's names.
∗ Make life-size paintings of the children and display them.

Links with home

Ask parents to send in photos of the children. Design a page for parents to complete with their child at home, such as 'What was I like as a baby?' or 'When did I start to walk?'

Diary for a week

Learning outcome

To develop an understanding of time passing.

Group size

Four to six children.

What you need

A selection of books and poems about the days of the week, such as *Starting School* by Janet and Allan Ahlberg (Penguin) and *Mr Wolf's Week* by Colin Hawkins (Mammoth), felt-tipped pens, large sheets of paper clipped to an easel.

Preparation

This activity should take place towards the end of the session for 10–15 minutes each day, for at least a week. Have the paper and pens ready and make sure the area is large enough to seat the whole group.

What to do

On Monday read a poem, story or song from your selection. Show the children an example of a diary and discuss how some people keep a diary to remind them of the things they have done. Explain that you would like the children to help you keep a diary by writing down what happens every day.

Ask the children if they know which day it is. Label the sheet 'Monday'. Write down what the children would like you to record for that day. You might include things such as a birthday in the group, a parent who is helping or someone who is away. When you have collected two or three sentences read the page through together. Choose two children each day to illustrate the page by drawing pictures to match the writing.

Repeat the process each day for one week. Encourage the children to develop the language of time by using words or phrases such as yesterday, today, tomorrow, last week, next week. Recite the days of the week with the children each time that you add something to the diary. Gradually the children will build up a collection of known songs, stories and rhymes about the days of the week.

Questions to ask

Can you remember what we wrote yesterday? Do you think that will happen again tomorrow? What do we do in our group every day? What do you think that we should write down today that is really important? Who isn't here with us today?

For younger children

Carry out the activity in a small group of six to eight children. Limit the recording to one event each day.

For older children

Encourage older children to keep individual daily diaries in the form of zigzag books.

Follow-up activities

∗ Make a group diary with paintings of 'Things we do on Monday'.
∗ Keep a group attendance register using individual name cards.

Links with home

Ask the children's families to talk about the things they do on Saturdays and Sundays. Suggest that they discuss some of the similarities and differences between the things they do in the group and the things they do at home.

Do you remember when?

Learning outcome

To learn to sequence events in time and to talk about events that have hapened.

Group size

Six to eight children.

What you need

A collection of photographs of group activities that have taken place over a period of time, card, glue, paper, marker pen.

Preparation

Individually mount five or six photographs onto card. These should include pictures of the children, visitors to the group, events and pictures of the children engaged in activities such as in the role-play area and using the outside play equipment.

What to do

Show each photograph in turn to the children and encourage them to talk about what they can see and what they remember about the pictures. Ask each child in turn to describe what they recall and what they liked or disliked about the activity or event. Write down the things that they say.

When all the children have had a turn, mount the pictures with their comments as part of a display or make a scrapbook.

Use the finished collection to show visitors the range of activities that happen within the group.

Questions to ask

Can you remember when...? Which picture do you specially like? Tell me the names of all the people in this picture? How old were you when this photo was taken? Can you remember what happened next? How did you feel?

For younger children

Carry out this activity with a small group of three to four children. Reduce the number of photographs to three.

For older children

Ask the children to sequence the events in order. Discuss other factors associated with the photographs such as the time of year, season and so on. Ask the children to recall a recent event and draw or paint a picture.

Follow-up activities

* Build up a collection of annotated photo scrapbooks of significant events within the group.
* Ask the children to bring in a photo of a special time or event that they remember. Create a display of them.
* Make a photo diary of group activities over a two-week period.
* Help the children to take photos with a simple camera.

Links with home

Ask parents/carers to help prepare for this activity by talking about some of the things that the children can remember doing at the group.

Family photo

Group size
Four to six children.

What you need
The story 'A present for Granny' on page 79, photos of large and small family groups, such as wedding, holiday and birthday photos (some in frames). The photos should include old and young relatives and pets! Colouring materials, drawing paper, coloured and shiny paper, photocopiable page 89.

Preparation
Ask the children to bring in photos of their family if they can. Talk with the children about families and how families can vary in the way they are made up, in terms of number, age and gender. Some people may like to include their pets as family members. Explain that families may or may not live together. Draw the outline of a decorative picture frame onto a piece of paper for each child. Enlarge a copy of photocopiable page 89.

What to do
Read the story 'A present for Granny' to the whole group. This is about a family having their photo taken for a special occasion.

Discuss the illustrations and the story with the group. Show them your selection of family photos and discuss the enlarged picture on photocopiable page 89.

Ask the children if they can remember having their photo taken. Was it for a special occasion? Who else was in the photo?

Now ask the children to imagine that their family is going to have their photo taken for a special occasion. Give each child your prepared 'picture frame' piece of paper and ask them to draw a pretend photograph of their family inside the frame. Invite them to decorate their frames by cutting and sticking paper patterns around the edge. Discuss and display the finished pictures.

Questions to ask
Who will you put in your picture? What will s/he be wearing? Who is the tallest/ shortest person in your family? Is there anyone who is very old in your family?

For younger children
Work with younger children in smaller groups of three to four. Provide them with play people for them to put into family groups and role-play family situations.

For older children
Encourage older children to put a lot of detail in their drawings. Ask them to label some members of their family. Invite them to write a story about what they can see on the photocopiable page.

Follow-up activities
* Make pictorial family trees.
* Compile a variety of books about different families.
* Make individual zigzag information books about each child's family.
* Ask the children to draw a picture of the people who live in their house in order of height.

Growing up

Learning outcome

To understand that people change as they grow older and that families consist of different types of people.

Group size

Four to six children.

What you need

A selection of stories about families including *Titch* by Pat Hutchins (Red Fox), photographs of your own family including siblings and children if possible. Paints and large sheets of paper.

Preparation

Have the paper and paints ready to use.

What to do

Show the children photos of your family and talk about who the people are, their age and about the different relationships.

Read *Titch* to the children and show them the pictures. This is a story about the smallest member of the family coming to terms with his older siblings. Ask questions to help them focus on the differences between Titch and his brother and sister. Encourage the children to think about where they come in their families. Are they the youngest?

Invite the children to talk about the things they can do now compared to when they were babies. What things would they like to learn to do?

Now ask each child to paint a picture of one part of the story. Help them to think of a caption to go with their picture. When the paintings and captions are completed ask the children to help you to sequence them in the correct order. Display the paintings with captions at the children's eye level and encourage them to retell the story in their own words.

Questions to ask

What could Pete and Mary do that Titch couldn't? Why? What did Titch do really well? What will you be able to do when you are older?

For younger children

Work with the children in smaller groups and allow more time for individual discussion.

For older children

Make individual zigzag books, retelling the story with illustrations and captions.

Follow-up activities

∗ Provide play people for the children to sort in order of size and family relationships.
∗ Make a simple block graph showing how many people live in the children's homes.

Links with home

Invite one or two adults to bring in photos or videos of their child from birth to the present day, and talk about how they have changed.

Happy Birthday to me

Learning outcome

To begin to understand the sequence of months and the significance of birthdays.

Group size
Four to six children.

What you need
The song 'Birthday song' on page 86, large piece of card (A1 size), paper, felt-tipped pens, coloured pencils, crayons.

Preparation
Over a period of time celebrate the children's individual birthdays.

Encourage them to bring in birthday cards and a present to show. Sing the birthday song. Draw 12 colourful birthday cakes, one for each month of the year and display them as a birthday chart (see below). Cut out enough candle shapes for each child in the group to have one. Let the children decorate the cakes with patterns. Label the cakes with the names of the months, so that each cake represents a different month.

What to do
Ask the children if they know when their birthdays are. Are they in the summer or are they at Christmas time? Many children will not know the month of their birthday.

Explain that everyone has a special month in which they were born, and that once every year they celebrate that special day. Every time we have a birthday we are one year older. Say the names of the months together.

Show the children the chart and explain that each child will choose a candle shape, colour it in, write their name and stick it onto the correct birthday cake for their month.

Show the finished chart to the whole group and draw their attention to it each time a child has a birthday.

Questions to ask
Which month has the most/fewest birthdays? Are there any months with no birthdays? How old will you be on your next birthday? Can you find your friend's birthday?

For younger children
Younger children will need individual support for much of this activity.

For older children
Display the birthdays chart in a circle to show that it is a cyclical process. Do some practical addition and subtraction work by adding and taking away candles from a cake.

Follow-up activities
∗ Make play dough birthday cakes with the appropriate number of candles.
∗ Make party hats/ invitations for the home corner and encourage the children to role-play a birthday party.
∗ Design a birthday card for a friend/ member of family.

Links with home

Invite parents and carers to come in and help their child to find their birthday month on the chart. Invite them to join in their child's birthday celebrations.

Last week, this week, next week

Learning outcome

To sequence events in time.

Group size

Whole group.

What you need

Three large pieces of card labelled 'last week', 'this week' and 'next week', string or ribbon, circular pieces of card or paper to hang from the large pieces of labelled card, felt-tipped pens, pencils, crayons.

Preparation

Over a period of time familiarise the children with the concept of past, present and future by regular discussion of what they did before, what they are doing now and what they will do next.

What to do

Work with small groups of four to six children at a time. Show them the labelled cards and explain what they mean. With the children, talk about the things that happened in the group last week. Choose one event and write it down on a circular piece of card. Hang it from the 'last week' card. Do the same for 'this week'.

Now ask the children to predict what might happen next week. Once more write down one of their ideas on a circular piece of card and hang it from 'next week'. Ask the children to each draw a different picture to go with the writing on the circles of card. Cut out and stick these pictures with the writing. Repeat the activity in small groups until all the children have had a turn.

Hang the completed cards on the wall as a simple timeline and use them as an opportunity to reinforce the vocabulary and to discuss the range of past events and predictions.

Questions to ask

What have you done this week? What will you choose next week? What things do you like to do most in the group?

For younger children

Work with smaller groups of only two to four children. Concentrate on helping the children to understand the terms, yesterday, today and tomorrow.

For older children

Encourage the children to write the labels for the cards.

Follow-up activities

∗ Provide ways for the children to record their participation in an activity, such as putting their name cards in a pot or wallet.
∗ Make simple zigzag books about the past, present and future.

Links with home

Provide each child with an activity card. Ask parents to help their child to choose an activity each day that they would like to work at. Record this on the card at the beginning of each session.

Learning to talk

Learning outcome

To develop an understanding of how we learn to talk.

Group size

Six to eight children.

What you need

A collection of poems, stories and songs about babies including 'Laura' by Michael Rosen on page 76, a recording of babies and toddlers talking, tape-recorder.

Preparation

Set up the tape-recorder and have the poem 'Laura' to hand.

the ways the children now speak. Ask the children to suggest ways of helping very young children to learn to talk.

Questions to ask

Which was the first word that you said? How do babies tell their Mums or Dads if they are hungry or upset? What do young children do when they want something that they don't know the word for?

For younger children

Work with smaller groups of children. Encourage them to role-play parents and babies in the home corner.

What to do

Seat the children around the tape-recorder in a quiet area. Tell them that they are going to listen to very young children talking. Ask them to listen very carefully as you play the tape. Ask the children to tell you what they think. Now play the tape again, this time stopping after short intervals to discuss what the toddlers might be saying.

Now read the poem 'Laura' by Michael Rosen on page 76. Encourage children with younger siblings to talk about how younger children try to communicate their needs. Explain that when babies are learning to talk they often invent special words for people, toys, food and so on. Ask the children to tell you if they used any special words when they were babies. Make a list of them. Share the special words and names and talk about the changes in

For older children

Help the children to make a tape-recording of their speech. Encourage them to compare their speech with that of the babies and toddlers.

Follow-up activities

∗ Invite a Health Visitor or Speech Therapist to talk to the children about learning to talk.
∗ Set up a recording corner with tapes and a tape-recorder.
∗ Make some 'baby' puppets.
∗ Provide a variety of baby dolls for the role-play area.

Links with home

Before the activity make a simple questionnaire for the children to take home and complete with their parents. Use simple questions such as: What was the first word that I said? Did I have any special names for anyone? and so on.

When I was one

Learning outcome

To learn about how people change as they grow up.

Group size

Four to six children.

What you need

A selection of pictures of young children of different ages, a selection of songs/poems/rhymes about growing up including 'The End' by A A Milne in *Now We are Six* (Mammoth).

Preparation

Have the pictures and poem to hand.

What to do

Seat the children in a circle and read the poem to them. Ask them to discuss what they could and couldn't do when they were babies, how they have changed and what they can do now.

Explain to the children that together, you are going to play a circle game. Start with 'being one', and ask each child in turn to say what they were like or what they could do. For example, 'When I was one I could only crawl.' Continue one year at a time until you reach the age of the oldest children. Next try talking about the future, 'When I am six I will be able to ride my bike without stabilisers.'

Read or tell the children some stories or poems from your selection. Repeat the game, this time saying, 'When I was one I couldn't... now I can.'

Questions to ask

What could you do when you were only one-year-old? What will you be able to do next year?

For younger children

Concentrate on distinguishing between the past and the present with these children. Help them to remember something that they couldn't do when they were babies, that they are able to do now.

For older children

Extend the circle game by asking each child in turn to throw a dice into the middle of the circle. Ask them to count the number of dots thrown on the dice and talk about the corresponding age.

Follow-up activities

* Make a display of 'Things I could do when...' for each year of the children's lives.
* Paint pictures of babies and toddlers

Links with home

Ask the children to bring in some of the things that they used to use when they were babies. Make a display of them.

chapter five

Living things

In this chapter the children will be encouraged to explore and recognise the features of living things. They will be helped to make comparisons and recognise similarities and differences between themselves, other animals and plants.

I've got a body

Learning outcome

To be able to name and correctly position parts of the body.

Group size

Six to eight children.

What you need

Two large pieces of card, the song 'I've got a body' on page 83, card, paints, Blu-Tack, paper.

Preparation

Draw round the outline of a child onto a large piece of card. Paint it, adding eyes, mouth, hair, nose and so on. Cut out the body, and cut that into sections so that you are left with a separate torso, head, two legs, two arms, two hands and two feet. Mount the torso onto another large piece of card.

What to do

Seat the children in a circle. Show them the body pieces and ask the children to name them.

Sing the song 'I've got a body', making sure that you have a verse for each of the cut-out body parts (you can make up verses if required). Now sing the song again, stopping at the end of each verse to ask a child to select the appropriate body part and Blu-Tack it onto the body in the correct position. When all the body parts have been used, sing the song again, this time removing the correct body parts at the end of each relevant verse.

Now ask the children to paint individual pictures of themselves including all the body parts in the song. Display the paintings around the card model and label the body parts of the model.

Questions to ask

How many hands/feet/legs/arms do we need to stick on? Do you look the same as the card child? Is your hair the same colour?

For younger children

Provide some dolls for them to handle. Encourage them to name the body parts. Can they find them on their own bodies as well?

For older children

Make jointed people using card, paper, paint and split pins. Suspend them from the ceiling on a line of string.

Follow-up activities

∗ Make a collection of books, songs, poems and stories about the body.
∗ Look at bodies of other animals. What do they have that we don't?
∗ Write a body poem, beginning with the words: 'With my hands I can...'.

Links with home

Ask parents to talk about body parts with the children as they get dressed. For example, 'Two arms for your T-shirt'.

Home for a minibeast

To observe and record findings from a minibeast hunt.

Group size

Four to six children.

What you need

An outside area, such as a garden containing rocks, stones, wood and so on. A selection of books about minibeasts, several sets of plastic minibeasts, sand tray with sand, bark chippings, leaves, stones, pieces of wood, bug pots, pooters, soft paintbrushes, magnifying lens.

Preparation

Show the children the books about minibeasts and encourage discussion. Encourage the children to think positively about spiders, ants and beetles and try to dispel any fears of them. Tell the children that you are going on a minibeast hunt, but they must be very careful with the creatures because they are very fragile. Show the children how to collect the minibeasts gently using a soft paintbrush or pooter. Introduce the idea of caring for small creatures. Explain that when you have collected the minibeasts and looked closely at them you will put them back exactly where they came from.

What to do

Take each group in turn to the outside area and help them to look carefully under stones, rocks, fallen branches and leaves. Help them to collect some of the creatures and to observe their appearance and the way in which they move. Do they know the name of their creature? Put the minibeasts back where they were found.

When all the children have had a turn, help them to make a minibeast environment in a sand tray or large plastic container using the bark chippings, sand, rocks and pieces of wood.

At a time when the children are not in the room, place the plastic minibeasts into the play environment. Now prepare for the excitement when they are found!

Questions to ask

How many legs do you think it has? Which part is its head? Can you point to its eyes? What do you think it eats?

For younger children

Work in smaller groups of two to four children. Encourage vocabulary of size, speed and position.

For older children

Provide clipboards, paper and pencils and encourage them to draw the minibeasts that they find.

Follow-up activities

∗ Complete photocopiable page 90. The children have to make combinations of eight dots on the ladybirds' wings.
∗ Make a minibeast book encouraging the children to make up some of their own minibeasts.
∗ Make play dough minibeasts.
∗ Read to children the story *The Very Hungry Caterpillar* by Eric Carle (Penguin).
∗ Keep stick insects as group pets.

Links with home

Ask parents to encourage positive responses to insects and small creatures, and to look for them in and around the home environment.

Where's my mummy?

Learning outcome

To recognise that baby animals often look like their parents.

Group size

Six to eight children.

What you need

Pictures of well-known adult animals and their young, including a human adult and baby (for example, a chicken, cow, pig, horse and sheep), two sheets of A3 sugar paper, felt-tipped pens, glue, strips of Velcro, clear adhesive film, card, scissors.

Preparation

Make a book by folding two sheets of A3 sugar paper. Write on the title, 'Where's my mummy?'. On the top half of each page stick a picture of an adult animal, on the bottom half glue a piece of Velcro. Mount the baby animal pictures on pieces of A5 card. Glue pieces of Velcro to the back of each piece of card.

What to do

Seat the children around the book with the baby cards nearby. Tell the children that you have made a book about animals, but that you need help to put the baby animals on the right page with their mummy.

Ask each child to choose a card and say the name of the animal that they have chosen. Now with each child in turn start at the beginning of the book and go through until the child thinks that s/he has found the right page. Do the rest of the group agree? Ask him/her to stick the baby under the mother.

When all the cards have been used up read the book with the children, discussing the similarities and differences between the baby and mother, including the human examples.

Leave the book and cards in a place where the children can choose to play the matching game independently.

Questions to ask

Why do you think she is his mummy? What is the same about the mummy and the baby? What is different? How has the mummy changed since she was a baby? Do you know of any baby animals that don't look like their mummy or daddy?

For younger children

Give the children plenty of help to match the mothers and babies. Point out specific features that are the same to help them match the correct pairs.

For older children

Introduce animals and their babies who are very different, such as caterpillars and butterflies.

Follow-up activities

∗ Play animal lotto.
∗ Make animal 'snap' cards with pictures of animals and their young.
∗ Complete the activity sheet on page 91, to match up pictures of baby animals with their mothers.

Links with home

Let the children take home their completed activity sheets to share their knowledge with the people at home.

Who lives here?

Learning outcome

To recognise that living things live in a variety of habitats.

Group size
Four to six children.

What you need
Card, felt-tipped pens, glue and spreaders, pictures of a variety of animals, birds, fish and insects and pictures of their habitats.

Preparation
Have ready a large piece of card and the pictures of the animals and their corresponding habitats.

What to do
Explain to the children that they are going to make a guessing game about animals and their homes for other children to play.

Ask each child in turn to choose an animal from the set of animal pictures and then to find its home in the 'homes' set. They should then stick the picture down onto the large piece of card and cover it with the matching 'home' card by putting glue on the top of the card and sticking it over the picture so that it will open as a flap.

When each child has had a turn, look at the animals and their homes and talk about the similarities and differences they can spot.

Now ask the children to suggest other animals and their habitats. Repeat the process introducing different animals and habitats with each group. The completed pictures can now be used as a game or as a display on a wall at the children's height.

Questions to ask
Can you match the spider to his home? What is the name of it? What do you think birds use to make a nest? Do you know of any animals who dig their homes underground? Which animals live in water?

For younger children
Work in small groups. Allow the children some time to play with plastic animals and puppets and let them have plenty of discussion time.

For older children
Make individual 'flap' books of animals and their homes.

Follow-up activities
∗ Make habitats with wet sand, sticks, shoe boxes and so on.
∗ Look closely at and paint a picture of a spider's web.
∗ Paint some pictures of the children's homes with flaps for doors, windows and so on.
∗ Make a book about the different types of homes that people live in today and in the past.
∗ Complete the activity sheet on page 92. Draw an animal for each home.

Complete the activity sheet on page 92.

Links with home
Ask parents or carers to accompany you on a visit to your local park, woods or river to look out for animals in their natural settings.

The pet shop

Learning outcome

To understand that living things need certain conditions in which to thrive.

Group size

Four to six children.

What you need

Photos and posters of pets, soft toys, a role-play area set up as a pet shop or pet clinic, paper, paints, felt-tipped pens. A visitor who works with animals.

Preparation

Invite a visitor, for example, an assistant at the local vets or pet shop, to talk to the children about his/her job working with animals. Ask the visitor to discuss caring for pets.

Invite the children to bring in photos of their pets if possible and have ready a selection of photos of usual and unusual pets. Set up the role-play area as a pet shop or clinic.

Ask the children to paint or draw a picture of their chosen pet on paper. Ask each child individually to say one thing about the care of their chosen animal, such as, 'Dogs need to go for a walk every day'. Encourage each child to have a go at writing a caption for their picture. You may wish to scribe afterwards underneath the child's writing.

When finished, help each child to stick the poster up in the 'Pet Shop'.

Questions to ask

What does your pet eat? Does it eat the same as you? What sort of pet would you choose if you could? How would you look after it?

For younger children

Use a choice of animal puppets or soft toys instead of photographs.

A pet is for life

What to do

Discuss the recent visit asking the children to recall what things pets need to help them to stay healthy and happy. Remind the children how important it is to know how to look after a pet before you buy one from the pet shop. Explain that as part of the 'Pet Shop' area, you need to make posters to help others learn how to look after their pets.

Show the group a selection of pet pictures and ask them to choose one to make a poster about. They may like to choose their own pet if they have one.

For older children

Make a book about caring for pets, written and illustrated by the children.

Follow-up activities

* Make a simple block graph of pets that belong to the children.
* Paint pictures of pets.
* Make a book of unusual pets such as a boa constrictor.

Links with home

Ask parents who have pets to talk to their child about the daily routines involved in looking after it.

What do you hear?

Learning outcome

To associate sounds with particular animals.

Group size

Six to eight children.

What you need

The book *Polar Bear, Polar Bear, What Do You Hear?* by Bill Martin and Eric Carle (Puffin), a selection of poems and songs about animals, such as 'Old MacDonald had a farm'.

Preparation

Have ready a copy of the book and gather the children in a group in front of you.

What to do

Read the story *Polar Bear, Polar Bear, What Do You Hear?* to the children. It is about two bears and the sounds they hear on their walk. Discuss the sounds that each animal made. Read the story again, asking the children to join in with each animal sound. Tell the children that you are going to play a circle game where they can choose an animal and make its sound. Can the children suggest other animals which are not in the story, and the sounds they make?

Use each child's name in turn and ask her/him what they can hear: 'Carla, Carla, what do you hear?' The child then chooses an animal and replies with the animal and its sound, 'I hear a duck quacking in my ear.'

Ask the other children in the group to make the sound suggested after each turn. Repeat until each child has been included. As the children become familiar with the game, suggest more unusual animals and ask the children to guess what sounds they make. Finish by singing a song such as 'Old MacDonald had a farm'.

Questions to ask

What sound do you think a beetle might make? Which animals make loud sounds/quiet sounds? What sounds do you make when you are happy/sad/angry?

For younger children

Allow time for play and discussion with small world animals before the game.

For older children

At the end of the activity encourage the children to repeat all the animals and sounds made by the group in sequence.

Follow-up activities

∗ Make a tape-recording of each group for the listening centre.
∗ Make a group book with animals the children have chosen.
∗ Make simple finger puppets of animals.
∗ Paint pictures of animals to go with the circle game.

Links with home

Invite parents in at the end of a session to listen to or take part in the game with their children.

How does your garden grow?

Learning outcome

To observe change in growing plants.

Group size

Whole group and then smaller groups.

What you need

An old sand or water tray or similar large rigid plastic container, rocks, pebbles, peat-free compost, a small bowl, grass seed, bedding plants, bulbs, water, camera, film, small trowels, watering can, gardening books, seed catalogues, the nursery rhyme 'Mary, Mary, quite contrary'.

Preparation

Teach the children the rhyme 'Mary, Mary, Quite Contrary'. Gather together the materials. Tell the children that together you are going to make an indoor garden. Explain that they will design, plant and care for the garden as it grows. Show the children books and pictures in small groups to help them decide what will be in their garden. Make a rota of children who will care for the garden.

What to do

Work with small groups of four to six children at a time, letting them fill the container with compost and positioning rocks, pebbles and a container for a pond. Suggest that the garden has several areas including a grassy area, a water garden, a rock garden and a flower garden.

When the design and building of the garden is complete ask each group of children to plant an area with bulbs and plants or to sow seed. Read out the instructions that come with the plants. What will they need? Ask the first two children on the rota to water the garden.

Help the children to take photographs of the whole process. Watch the garden grow and photograph the changes taking place. Mount the photos for display. As the plants die replace them with a seasonal variety. For example, plant daffodil bulbs in late autumn and nasturtiums in spring.

Questions to ask

What must we do to help the plants grow? What does the compost feel like? How many bulbs do you think we will need? How can we make the garden look more colourful?

For younger children

Construct the garden with small groups of two or three children. Allow them some time to play with the compost and rocks before they have to create the garden.

For older children

Make a book entitled 'Grow your own garden', written and illustrated by the children.

Follow-up activities

* Make some garden collages using seed catalogue pictures.
* Design the cover for a seed packet.
* Paint pictures of Mary's garden.
* Draw or paint observational pictures of plants or flowers.

Links with home

Tell the children's families about the garden by writing about it in your newsletter. Suggest how they might make a miniature garden at home using a seed tray.

Five little peas

Learning outcome

To notice similarities and differences between pea pods and to record findings.

Group size
Four children.

What you need

Fresh peas in pods, the rhyme 'Five little peas in a pea-pod pressed' see page 78, paper, coloured pencils.

Preparation

Put a selection of unopened garden pea-pods on a tray. Seat the children in a circle around the tray.

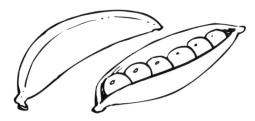

What to do

Say the rhyme 'Five little peas in a pea-pod pressed' two or three times, encouraging the children to join in when they are ready. Hand the pea-pods around for the children to look at, feel, and smell. Encourage them to describe their observations. What do they feel and smell like? Can they suggest what they might be?

Now explain to the children that there is something special inside the pea-pods, what might it be? Give each child their own pea-pod and show them how to open them carefully. Encourage the children to describe and guess what it is they find. Tell them that they are peas just like the ones they eat at home. Do the peas at home come out of pods or a packet? Now help each child in turn to count the peas in her/his pod. Who has the most/fewest?

Seat the group around a table and ask each child to draw the inside of her/his pea-pod. Finish by reciting the rhyme one more time.

Questions to ask

What do you think we might find inside? What do you like to eat with peas? Do the peas that you eat at home come out of a pod like this? Where do they come out of?

For younger children

Allow younger children plenty of time to investigate their pea pods before recording their observations.

For older children

Show the children how to use a magnifying lens, holding it close to the pea and not their eye. Ask them to notice any differences in what they can see with and without the lens.

Follow-up activities

* Grow pea plants in compost. Harvest and taste the peas.
* Plant mung beans or other beans that are quick to germinate and watch them grow together.
* Make a block graph to show the number of peas found in the pods.
* Soak dried peas or beans and observe the changes.

Links with home

Tell the children's families about your planned activity and ask them to try planting peas or beans at home with their child.

Autumn leaf hunt

Learning outcome

To recognise and sort leaves into a variety of shapes, sizes and colours.

Group size

Two to three children.

What you need

Local wooded area within walking distance, adult helpers, paper carrier bags for collecting leaves, first aid box, magnifying lenses.

Can the children find any animals living under the leaves?

On your return, ask each group including the adults to tip out their leaves, sort them in a variety of ways and examine them closely. Provide each group with a magnifying lens. What do they notice about the leaves? Record one observation from each group on a large piece of paper, such as: 'Simon noticed that one of his leaves has three different colours on it.'

Preparation

You will need to ensure that there is a high ratio of adults to children for safety and a successful experience. Aim for at least one adult for every two children. Invite the helpers to come in before the walk and talk to them about your expectations and the purpose of the walk. Remind them of safety precautions. Give the helpers some examples of questions they could ask and what to look out for. Tell them which children they will be responsible for. Always ensure that you carry a first aid box with you on an outing.

What to do

Explain to the children that the leaves are falling from the trees because it's autumn. Give each group a carrier bag and ask them to collect leaves of different shapes, sizes and colours. Look up at the sky noticing how the trees are growing up towards the light. Listen for noises including the leaves crunching underfoot. Lift the leaves up, letting them flutter to the ground.

Questions to ask

Which is the largest/smallest leaf? How many different colours/shapes can you find? What will happen to the trees when spring comes? What do the leaves feel like?

For younger children

Concentrate on developing vocabulary to help them describe what they see, feel, hear and smell.

For older children

Ask the children to sort the leaves in different ways, into sets of size, shape and colour.

Follow-up activities

* Make leaf rubbings and leaf prints.
* Make a woodland collage using natural materials.

Links with home

Ask parents or carers to encourage their children to notice seasonal changes on their way to and from the group.

Blooming bulbs

Learning outcome

To observe and record the changes in a growing bulb.

Group size
Four children.

What you need
Hyacinth bulbs in spring or other seasonal bulbs, two transparent hyacinth pots, water, plastic magnifying lenses.

Preparation
Have ready a weekly rota of children in fours, an observation and recording chart, the bulbs and pots. Make an observation chart which is divided into weeks.

What to do
Show the children the pots and bulbs. Pass the bulbs around the group and encourage the children to describe what they can see and feel. Explain that you are going to fill the pots with water and place the bulbs in the top section with the bottom of the bulbs touching the water. Place the bulbs carefully and ask the children to predict what they think will happen next.

Show the children the observation chart and explain that they will take turns in groups of four, on the same day each week, to look closely at the bulbs and draw a picture of what they can see. Explain that their recordings will be stuck onto the chart so that they can see if there is a change and when it has happened. Choose four children to start the chart by drawing the bulb. Continue the activity over a planned period of time. Encourage the children to discuss their observations, suggest why changes are happening and predict what might happen next.

Questions to ask
Why are the roots growing down into the water? What would happen if we didn't keep the pot filled with water? What patterns/colours can you see when you look closely at the bulb?

For younger children
Take photographs of the bulbs as they grow to give younger children a clearer visual picture of the way the bulb has changed. They will need close adult support in order to notice the fine details.

For older children
Encourage the children to take greater responsibility for watering the pot and making observations.

Follow-up activities
* Try growing an avocado pip suspended over water by pins.
* Grow mustard and cress seeds on a variety of surfaces, such as tissue, cotton wool, blotting paper and peat-free compost.
* Plant different seeds in the compartments of empty cardboard egg boxes. Record what happens.
* Plant bulbs in pots or in the ground outside.

Links with home
Ask adults to collect containers and to donate a variety of bulbs and seeds.

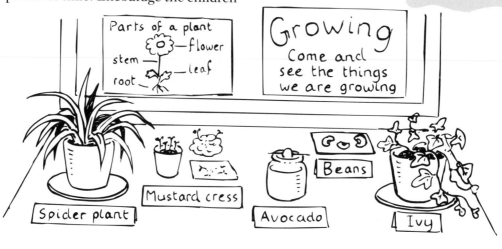

chapter six

Exploring our environment

In this chapter the activities focus on the local environment. Children are encouraged to become aware of a variety of features in their local area and their purposes. They are helped to record their observations through talk, modelling and drawing.

Out and about

Learning outcome

To be aware of some of the features of the local environment.

Group size
Six children.

What you need
A large piece of frieze paper, a display area, paper, paints, crayons, pencils, scissors, glue.

Preparation
Arrange a short walk in the local area. Choose a walk that passes a variety of features such as shops, houses, a green space and a church. Have a ratio of one adult to two children and ask the adults to remind the children to listen as well as look, and to look up as well as down. Allow plenty of time for the walk so that the children are not rushed.

What to do
Back indoors, gather together a small group of children. Ask each child to recall what they noticed on the walk. Record the children's comments into sets of 'What we saw/what we heard'.

Prompt the children with questions that will help to develop their descriptive vocabulary and positional language: 'Tell me about the church. Was it taller than the houses next to the shops? What do you think it was made from?'

Now ask each child to paint one feature of the walk, such as a house. Encourage the children to include as much detail as possible. When all the pictures are complete, help the children to position them side by side on a large piece of paper to make a frieze. Repeat the process until every child has had a turn. Now write a caption for the picture entitled 'On our walk'. Display at the children's level.

Questions to ask
What did we notice at the beginning of the walk? What sounds did we hear? What things can you buy from the shops that we saw?

For younger children
Provide plenty of opportunities for younger children to talk about the walk, recalling significant features. Help them to add detail to their paintings through discussion.

For older children
Focus upon and develop one particular aspect of the walk, for example how many kinds of homes did we see? (Flats, terraced houses, nests and so on.)

Follow-up activities
∗ Make a street with construction toys and small world people.
∗ Paint pictures of individual homes.
∗ Make a 'How we travel to school' graph and draw pictures of the different ways.

Links with home

Ask parents to talk with their child about what they see and hear on the way to the group. Encourage as many adults as possible to join you on the walk.

Weather bear

Group size

Whole group or smaller group.

What you need

Teddy bear and items of clothing in a variety of materials including waterproof clothing, the 'Weather bear' poem from page 77, a selection of poems and songs about the weather – 'Weather' by Linda Mort and Janet Morris in the *Themes for early years* series (Scholastic) is a useful source.

Preparation

Have the poem to hand. Place a bear and a variety of clothes in a special place such as on the wall, a shelf or in a special basket. Prepare a rota with the children's names on a piece of card for taking turns to dress the bear.

What to do

Read the poem 'Weather Bear' to the children. Show them the teddy and each item of clothing. Encourage the children to describe the clothes and to suggest in which weather they might be worn.

Take the children outside or look through a window at the weather. Ask them to describe the weather and talk about the clothes they need to wear for that type of weather. Now select the most appropriate clothes for the bear.

Show the children the rota and explain that they will all take it in turns to dress the teddy in the right clothes for the weather. Choose two children

to go first and ask them to dress the teddy. Display the teddy in the special place.!"

Finish by reading the 'Weather Bear' poem to the children again. Repeat the activity several times each week over a planned period of time.

Questions to ask

How do you feel today? (Hot, cold, wet, dry?) What will you wear when you go out today? What clothes did you bring with you today? Do you need an umbrella or wellington boots today?

For younger children

Carry out this activity in a group of four to six children. Allow time to play with the bear, dressing and undressing him before discussion.

For older children

Watch a weather forecast on television to stimulate role-play. Make weather symbols using card and paints to stick onto a large outline map of the UK.

Make a simple pictorial weather chart to represent the pattern of the weather for one week using photocopiable page 93.

Follow-up activities

* Collect snow in a bucket to bring in and observe the changes.
* Make a collection of different clothes for the home corner.
* Paint pictures about the weather. Make a display of them.

Moving house

Learning outcome

To recognise people's needs in their environment.

Group size

Six children.

What you need

A doll's house and furniture, play people, a variety of modelling materials, felt-tipped pens, glue, paper, paint, scissors.

Preparation

Discuss with the children where they sleep at home, who shares their bedroom and what furnishings, toys and equipment they have. Make a list of things including all the children's contributions. Have ready the empty doll's house, furnishing and dolls.

Be sensitive to individual children's backgrounds.

What to do

Tell the children that you are going to pretend that the family of dolls are moving house. Explain that they need to help the play children choose a bedroom in the house and put in all the things the play children will need or want. Help the children to select appropriate furnishings from the doll's house set.

Next, refer to the list and suggest to the children that they make extra furnishings and toys with the modelling materials. For example, they may wish to make a television, bedspread, computer and so on using small boxes, paper and felt-tipped pens. When the room has been furnished, invite the play children to take up residence! Repeat the activity assigning each group a different room in the house.

Questions to ask

How many children will be sharing the bedroom? How many beds will we need? In which room shall we put the children's toys? What can we use to make a television or computer?

For younger children

Allow more time for play, discussion and development of appropriate vocabulary.

For older children

Ask each group of children to draw and label a picture of their own bedroom.

Follow-up activities

* Make a collage picture for each room using pictures from catalogues and magazines.
* Over a period of time reorganise the role-play area as a different room. Make furniture and toys using modelling materials, various boxes, paints, paper and glue.

Links with home

Ask the children's families to describe their own childhood bedrooms and suggest that they compare similarities and differences between then and now.

Playing in the park

Learning outcome

To observe and record features of a play area in the community.

Group size

Four children.

What you need

The story 'A visit to the park' on page 82, a local park or play area with a variety of equipment, a large sand tray, wet and dry sand, construction toys such as LEGO or Duplo, small world toys including play figures, a selection of natural and manufactured modelling materials such as fir cones, pebbles, lollipop sticks, art straws, ribbon, cotton reels, foil containers, string, adhesive, scissors.

Preparation

Visit a local park or play area with the group, making sure that there are plenty of adult helpers.

What to do

Gather the children together in a small group. Read the story 'A visit to the park'. Ask the children to talk about what they enjoyed playing with at the park. Ask them to try and think of ways to make the park even better such as by having more swings, a pond or a bouncy castle.

Allow plenty of time for the group to play with the sand and toys and to explore the materials provided. Now explain that you would like them to work together to make a park for the toys in the sand area. Encourage the children to reproduce their own ideas from the earlier discussion, selecting appropriate materials from the collection. When the park is ready, organise a special opening ceremony for the toys.

When the group has had a day or two to play with the park repeat the process with another group.

Questions to ask

How can we make an area for the toys to sail their boats? What can we use to make a shady place? How many swings do the toys need? Can we find something to make a see-saw?

For younger children

Allow more time for play with construction toys and small world people before the activity.

For older children

Ask the children to draw an imaginary park including features that they would like to build in the play park.

Follow-up activities

* Discuss where and how to play safely in the community.
* Build a play enclosure with blocks.
* Make a see-saw using big blocks and planks.

Links with home

Invite parents or carers to accompany their child on the group outing to the park or to follow up with their own visit on a separate occasion.

Let's go shopping

Learning outcome

To be aware of the purpose and features of shops in the local area.

Group size

Six to eight children.

What you need

Adult helpers – a ratio of one adult to two children is ideal, an appropriate shop such as a supermarket/bakers/greengrocers, a small amount of money to make some purchases, shopping bags, paper, pencils.

Preparation

Contact the shop before the visit so that they are prepared. If possible, ask for an assistant to be available to talk to the children.

What to do

Tell the children that they will all be visiting a shop in small groups over the next few days. Ask them what they think they will be able to buy. Allocate one to two children to each adult helper. At the shop encourage the children to look carefully at the goods on sale and to ask questions about how the food is kept clean and fresh.

Give each child a small amount of money and encourage all the children to purchase one item to take back to share with the group, such as an apple or some biscuits.

On your return, gather all the children together to listen to the 'shoppers" account of their visit and to share their purchases. If possible ensure that different groups visit different types of shops and encourage discussion of similarities and differences between the shops.

Questions to ask

Do the apples all look the same? Where do you think this food comes from? Which cake is the largest/smallest? Which people are selling/buying things? What is in that tin? How do you know?

For younger children

Have a ratio of one adult to one child, with younger children.

For older children

Tell the children in advance which sort of shop they will be visiting, and help them to write shopping lists to take with them.

Follow-up activities

∗ Create a shop in the role-play area.
∗ Make and bake play dough biscuits and cakes.
∗ Design and make simple shopping bags.
∗ Paint advertisements for fruit, cakes and so on.

Links with home

Ask parents to involve their child in a visit to the shops by making shopping lists, finding items at the shop and helping to put away the shopping together.

The health centre

Learning outcome

To learn about the local health centre using knowledge from personal experience.

Group size
Eight to ten children.

What you need
Reclaimed modelling materials, boxes, paint, paper, felt-tipped pens, crayons, glue, scissors.

Preparation
Contact your local health centre and arrange a visit. Many health centres are keen to encourage children to develop positive attitudes to healthy living and if plenty of advance notice is given, it may be possible to arrange for a practice nurse to talk to the children. Ask him or her to explain why parents and children might visit a health centre.

Prior to the visit encourage the children to talk about their experiences at a health centre. Make a list of the variety of reasons for going to the health centre – to have an injection, to weigh the baby, to see a doctor when you are not well. Gather together the materials needed to make a variety of equipment for a role-play health centre.

What to do
During the visit, encourage the children to ask questions and draw their attention to the features of the centre such as posters on the wall, a reception area, weighing scales, computers and so on.

When you are back at your group suggest that the children make a health centre for the toys. Encourage suggestions of what you could make for

the centre. Help the children to set up a reception area equipped with play phones, a computer or typewriter, paper, pens and pencils, an area for the baby clinic with a bed and weighing scales and a doctor's area with prescriptions, pads and pencils. Equip the centre with bandages, make stethoscopes and 'Staying Healthy' posters to display in the centre. When the play health centre is complete, invite someone from your local health centre to visit.

Questions to ask
How do people know when it is their turn to see the doctor? Why do babies come to see the health visitor? Who do you meet first when you arrive at the centre? What does the receptionist do? Who wears special clothes or uniforms? What do doctors have in their cases?

For younger children
Concentrate on fewer features both on the visit and when creating the role-play area.

For older children
Ask older children to write letters to the people at the Health Centre, thanking them for their help and allowing them to visit.

Follow-up activities
∗ Take photos of the visit and the children's role-play and make a large book with captions.
∗ Paint pictures for a healthy food display.
∗ Collect a list of local GPs and map the children's names to their GP.

Links with home

Ask parents to discuss with their child any routine check-ups and inoculations they may have had and why.

Looking up

Learning outcome

To observe, describe and record what is seen when we look up.

Group size

Six to eight children.

What you need

A fine but cloudy day, paper, paints, collage materials, glue, pieces of sponge.

Preparation

Tell the children that you are all going to go outside to look at the sky. Explain that it is very dangerous to look at the sun because it can hurt our eyes. Ensure that the children are suitably dressed.

What to do

Take the children outside to an area with trees and shrubs if possible. Ask them to lie down on their backs in a circle with their eyes closed and heads pointing in.

Touch each child in turn and ask him to describe one thing that he notices, saying 'When I look up I can see...'. Repeat this process one more time.

Go back inside with the children and sponge print a large piece of paper a 'sky' colour. Ask each child to paint a large picture of one thing she or he noticed such as a cloud, bird or tree. Encourage the children to describe what they see as they paint. Repeat the process with each group.

Display and label the finished picture with appropriate captions.

Questions to ask

What do you think the clouds would feel like if you could touch them? What colour is the sky today? What shapes did you notice when you looked at the leaves and buildings?

For younger children

Reduce the group size to four. Allow more time for discussion and repeat the game outside three or four times.

For older children

Ask the children to make individual pictures of the things they saw or the things they think they might see when they look up.

Follow-up activities

* Look up indoors. Record what you see and compare it with the things that you saw outside.
* Play an outside listening game with eyes closed.
* Make a collection of pictures of aeroplanes and birds.

Links with home

Explain the activity to the children's families and ask them to help their child to describe what they see at home, in the garden, or from a window.

Where is Fred?

Learning outcome

To look carefully at and describe features of the group's environment.

Group size

Four to six children.

What you need

A soft toy to take on the role of 'Fred' (or any other name that you choose).

language by encouraging them to ask questions such as: 'Is he hiding in the cupboard?' or 'Is he hiding on top of the books?'

Preparation

Gather the children together. Ensure that they are all able to see the different parts of the room.

What to do

Introduce 'Fred' to the children and explain that he wants to play a game of hide-and-seek. Ask the children if they have ever played hide-and-seek. Have a discussion about what you do when you play it. Explain that Fred is going to hide somewhere in the setting and ask the children to help him to think of some good places to hide.

Explain to the children that they will all have a turn to hide Fred, but that they must not look when someone else is hiding him. Each time that Fred is being hidden say a popular rhyme together. When a child has hidden Fred invite the other children to ask questions to find out where he is hiding. The child who hid Fred has to answer 'Yes' or 'No'. Use the opportunity to develop the children's positional

Questions to ask

Provide examples for the children to follow, such as: Is he under the paint table? Is he in the cloakroom? Can you remember all the places that Fred hid today?

For younger children

Younger children will need adult help to find a suitable place to hide Fred. They will also need help with naming parts and objects in the setting.

For older children

Make a book about the places that Fred has hidden. Invite the children to draw pictures of Fred and give them help to write the captions if necessary.

Follow-up activity

✻ Look at books that involve finding hidden objects or people such as *Where's Spot?* by Eric Hill (Picture Puffin).

Links with home

Tell parents or carers about the hide-and-seek game you have been playing and encourage them to practise the game at home. Explain that this will help to develop their child's positional vocabulary.

The bear went over the mountain

Learning outcome

To develop an awareness of features in the immediate environment and local area.

Group size

Six to eight children.

What you need

A toy bear or teddy bear, a simple drawing/painting of a mountain, an old curtain or large piece of material, the song 'The bear went over the mountain' on photocopiable page 84.

What to do

Teach the children the song 'The bear went over the mountain'. When the children are familiar with the song encourage them to act it out using the teddy bear and the picture of the mountain, or a mountain made with a cloth covering a large object.

Talk to the children about what their teddy bear would see if it went out of the door of their setting. Try and adapt the words of the song accordingly: 'The bear went out of the door... (repeat).
And all that he could see... was the houses and the trees (repeat).'

Gradually build up this 'song game' by taking the bear to different places such as 'into the kitchen' or 'round the corner'. Take the children with you to see what the teddy would see.

Questions to ask

What was on the other side of the mountain? What would you see if you went round the corner? What would you see if you went to the shoe shop?

For younger children

Restrict what the bear can see to features in the immediate setting. Encourage them to take the bear to the place and talk about what they can see.

For older children

Encourage them to be adventurous, including places in their local area and further afield. Write down some of their alternative verses in a big book for them to refer to when they are singing the song. Invite the children to illustrate the book.

Follow-up activities

✳ Take the bear for a walk round the immediate area and record everything that he saw in sequence. Draw pictures about his journey.
✳ Read the children stories about journeys.

Links with home

Ask the parents to make a list with their child of all the things that they see on their way from home to the group.

Playmats

Learning outcome

To become aware of some of the features of the local area.

Group size

Two to four children.

What you need

Large sheets of white paper or card, pencils, crayons, felt-tipped pens and paints, small vehicles, blocks and play people, a commercially produced playmat.

Preparation

In small groups with plenty of adult helpers, take the children for a walk around the local area. Talk to the children about the purpose of some of the places such as the shop, post office and garage.

What to do

Show the children the playmat and talk about the features that it shows. Remind the children about their walk around the area and talk about the things that they saw and what makes their own area special.

Explain that they are going to make their own playmats to show what it is like in their area. Help the children to start their own 'map' by drawing in some roadways together. Then ask them to select their own materials to draw, paint and colour in other features that they choose. Do not expect the playmat to represent the area exactly!

When their playmat is finished, encourage the children to use these for small world play using blocks to represent buildings and vehicles and play people to create activity.

Questions to ask

Where did you walk? What did you see on your walk? What do people do there? What will you put on your playmat?

For younger children

Make one big playmat. Draw in the roads for the children and ask them to choose one thing to paint or draw.

For older children

Some children may be able to make a playmat with a partner. Encourage them also to build model houses, vehicles and other features to use on the mat.

Follow-up activities

✳ Take photographs of features in the local area and make a display.
✳ Invite people from the local area to talk to the children about what they do and where they live and work.

Links with home

Produce a simple hand-out about features in the area that would be of interest to young children. Ask the children's families if they could find time to visit these with their children.

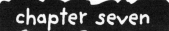

chapter seven

Objects and materials

In this chapter the activities have been chosen to support the children's development of scientific understanding. The activities will provide practical opportunities for the children to ask questions about how and why things happen while exploring materials and their properties.

Sorting the clothes

Learning outcome

To sort and select materials.

Group size
Six children.

What you need
An interesting selection of clothing representing clothes for hot and cold weather such as a straw hat, baseball cap, woollen scarf, fur-lined boots and so on. A large rubber dice, three pictures of the sun, three pictures of snowy weather, glue.

Preparation
Place the clothes in a large, low container. Stick the pictures onto the dice so that three sides represent hot weather and three represent cold.

What to do
Gather the children together in a circle. Show them the sunny pictures on the dice. Ask them to describe how they feel in hot, sunny weather. Now do the same with the snowy pictures.

Show the children each item of clothing, asking them to discuss whether it would be worn in hot weather or cold weather.

Now ask each child in turn to throw the dice into the middle of the circle. Ask them to look at the picture on the dice and choose an item of clothing that corresponds to the picture they have thrown on the dice. For example, 'Jane has thrown a sunny picture so she has

chosen the big straw hat.'

Repeat the game until all the clothes have been chosen. Finish by asking the children to say if they are wearing hot or cold weather clothes.

Questions to ask
Why wouldn't you wear the woolly jumper when it's hot? Are these sandals suitable for wearing in the snow? Why not? When might you wear a swimsuit on a snowy day? What would you take with you on a holiday to a hot or a cold country?

For younger children
Ensure that the clothes are limited to two items each and that they are easy to put on.

For older children
Include one or two items of clothing that might be suitable for either hot or cold weather, such as a shirt.

Follow-up activities
* Make a collection of books which show what people wear in hot/cold countries.
* Provide hot and cold weather clothes for role-play.
* Make collections of hot and cold weather clothes for the dolls and teddies.

Links with home

Ask carers to encourage their child to select appropriate clothing to wear each day.

Toast for Ted

Learning outcome

To observe the changes that happen to bread when it is toasted.

Group size
Four children.

What you need

A toaster, some sliced bread, a small table, chairs, cups, plates, plastic knives, butter or margarine, four teddies or dolls.

Preparation

Ask the children to help you to set up the role-play area ready to serve breakfast to the teddies. Discuss what the teddies might like to eat for breakfast.

the children put spread or butter on the toast and each invite a teddy for breakfast in the role-play area.

Questions to ask

How does the toast feel when you touch/squeeze it? What is the colour of the bread before/after you toast it? What happens when the hot toast begins to cool? What happens when we put spread on hot toast? How about cold toast?

For younger children

Limit the number of children to two for this activity.

What to do

Encourage the children to talk about their favourite breakfasts. Show them the bread and toaster and ask them to describe the bread and predict what will happen when it is heated in the toaster. Ensure that you observe the following health and safety points:

∗ Make sure that the children wash their hands before touching the food.

∗ Explain how dangerous it is to touch cooking equipment such as toasters.

∗ Remind the children not to try and make toast at home without an adult present.

Toast the bread and ask the children to notice the change that takes place. What differences can they notice between the bread and the toast? Let

For older children

Cut the toast into strips. Encourage the children to estimate how many 'soldiers' will be needed for each teddy to have 1, 2 or 3 each.

Follow-up activities

∗ Make a graph of favourite breakfasts.

∗ Make simple repetitive books starting with the phrase 'With my toast I like to eat...'.

∗ Make collage meals on paper plates using a variety of reclaimed materials.

∗ Make an instruction card for making toast.

∗ Design breakfast menus for the home corner.

Links with home

Ask the children's families to reinforce the work done in the group on safety in the kitchen.

Rolling down

Learning outcome

To begin to understand how things move.

Group size

Six children.

What you need

Construction toys with wheels such as LEGO or Duplo, a planed and sanded plank of wood, blocks.

Preparation

Over a period of time provide opportunities for the children to explore a variety of construction toys and large toys with wheels and help them to make vehicles.

Before the activity, have ready some wheeled toys that the children have made, several wooden blocks and a plank of wood.

What to do

Explain to the children that you are going to test the vehicles to see which ones will roll down the plank of wood. First, raise one end of the plank on blocks to make a slope (see below). Encourage each child to test his/her vehicle by rolling it down the slope. Discuss what happens with the children. For example, why do the children think some vehicles roll better than others?

Now vary the height of the slope by adding more blocks. Investigate and discuss what happens now. Finally, place the plank on the floor without blocks. Ask the children what they must do now to make the vehicles move. Investigate and discuss the outcome.

Perform this activity with all the children in small groups and allow them the opportunity to feed back their experiences to the whole group at a later time.

Questions to ask

What happens if we put a toy in the vehicle? Will the cars go faster or slower when we make the slope steeper? Is there any equipment in the park that you use to go down quickly?

For younger children

Allow plenty of opportunities for the children to play with large-wheeled toys such as bikes, prams and trolleys.

For older children

Investigate how large toys move on slopes and on flat surfaces. Encourage them to ask questions and make predictions.

Follow-up activities

∗ Use slopes with different textured surfaces such as carpet, shiny and wet surfaces.
∗ Put objects in front of and behind the vehicle. Discuss what happens.
∗ Investigate and compare movement down the slope with a selection of wheeled and non-wheeled toys.

Links with home

Ask parents or carers to talk with their children about other wheeled objects such as shopping trolleys and pushchairs.

Blowing bubbles

Learning outcome

To investigate bubble mixture and bubble shapes.

Group size

Four to six children.

What you need

Washing-up liquid, water, lengths of plastic-coated wire.

Preparation

Make a pot of bubble mixture by mixing washing-up liquid and water and have ready several lengths of plastic-coated wire approximately 15cm long for each child. Bend and twist the wire to make up a standard shaped wand with a round end for each child. Make sure that none of the children are allergic to washing-up liquid and that they are supervised closely when using the pieces of wire. Do not leave any sharp ends exposed.

What to do

Gather the children outside if the weather permits. Try to find an area that has a sheltered part and a windy part. Show the children how to dip the wand into the bubble mixture and make bubbles by blowing. Allow them time to investigate with their own wands and mixture.

Encourage the children to make observations and discuss what they are doing. Do the children notice what happens if they blow hard or gently? Can they make bubbles without blowing, for example by waving their wands?

Ask the children to observe the bubbles closely, noticing in particular the size, shape and colour of them.

Now experiment with making different shaped wands. Do the children think the shape of the bubbles will change to match the shape of the wand? Watch what happens.

Questions to ask

Do you know anything else that is the same shape as a bubble? What happens to the mixture after the bubble has burst? Are bubbles the same shape? Can we make them different? Are the bubbles the same colour as the mixture? Do the bubbles go up or down? What do bubbles feel like when you touch them?

For younger children

Reduce the group size to four children and concentrate on developing the language used to describe shape, size and movement of the bubbles.

For older children

Investigate different strengths of bubble mixture by varying the quantity of the washing-up liquid.

Follow-up activities

* Make a collection of spherical objects.
* Investigate other solutions that make bubbles.
* Make bubble prints.
* Make a group poem called 'Bubbles are...'.

Links with home

Tell the parents or carers about the activity and ask them to investigate different bubble mixtures with their child.

Making shadows

Learning outcome

To observe the similarities and differences between bodies, objects and their shadows.

Group size
Eight to ten children.

What you need

A sunny day, a concrete or a tarmac area, several large objects such as a chair, a bicycle, a large doll or teddy.

Preparation
Choose an area where shadows can be easily made and seen.

What to do
Gather the children together outside. Ask them to find a space close to but not touching a friend. Spend some time talking about the shadows that the children can make with their bodies. Can they make them move? Can they make the shadow's arm, head or leg move? Which parts of their body can they see on the shadow? Are any bits missing?

Encourage discussion that will help the children towards an understanding that the shadow they make is similar to their body and body parts, but not exactly the same. Now introduce the other objects and investigate the shadow patterns that they make.

With chalk, draw round one or two of the children's shadows. Ask them to lie on them. Do they fit? Now draw round a chair or bike and compare similarities and differences between the shadow outline and the object.

Questions to ask
Can you make your own shadow very big or very small? Can you catch your friend's shadow? Can you make the teddy's shadow wave? Can your shadow wave? What happens to shadows when a cloud passes in front of the sun?

For younger children
Concentrate on looking at the way they can move their own shadows. Can the children jump on their own shadow, or each other's?

For older children
Ask the children to suggest other things that would make good patterns.

Follow-up activities
∗ Try making patterns at different times of the day.
∗ Paint pictures of 'Me and my shadow'.
∗ Investigate making shadows with other light sources.
∗ Play at chasing each other's shadows.

Links with home

Explain the activity to the children's parents and ask them to follow up the activity by comparing their own shadow with their child's.

Whisk it up

Learning outcome

To observe what happens when you whisk different mixtures.

Group size

Four to six children.

What you need

A selection of whisks including a fork, a rotary whisk, a wire whisk, a bamboo whisk, egg whites, water, bath foam, oil and vinegar (six parts oil to one part vinegar), mixing bowls, aprons.

Preparation

Put the different mixtures into separate bowls and provide a bowl of plain water. Place the selection of the whisks on the table with the bowls. Check for allergies to substances such as bath foams.

What to do

Gather the children into a circle and ask them to put on aprons. Show them the whisks and pass them round the circle. Ask the children to suggest what the whisks might be used for.

Group the children in pairs around a large table with a plastic bowl and two to three whisks for each pair. Let the children experience whisking the plain water first. What happens if they whisk slowly or quickly? Do they notice the bubbles? What makes them? Now ask the children to try whisking the mixture in one of the other bowls. As they whisk the mixture, encourage them to talk about what is happening and note the similarities and differences between whisking the mixture and whisking the plain water. Let them compare the different types of mixture.

Questions to ask

Are there more bubbles than with the water? What is making them? Can you make more bubbles by whisking slowly or quickly? Why do you think the mixture is changing colour?

For younger children

Limit the activity to mixing varying amounts of bath foam with warm water to make a 'very bubbly bath'.

For older children

Ask the children to record what happened in four steps, by drawing pictures in each square of a piece of paper folded twice.

Follow-up activities

∗ Using bath foam and water compare the different whisks to see which is the most effective.
∗ Bathe some of the toys in bubble bath and plain water.
∗ Make a collection of kitchen utensils that whisk, beat, squeeze and stir. Ensure that they are safe for young children to handle.
∗ Create a role-play kitchen.

Links with home

Ask the children's families to emphasise safety in the kitchen at home. Suggest that one evening they allow their children to help them wash up the dirty dishes using water with and without washing-up liquid in for them to compare.

Fun with wheels

Group size

Six to eight children.

What you need

The song 'The wheels on the bus' on page 85, a collection of wheeled toys including small world, construction and large toys, pictures of things that have wheels such as vehicles, trolleys, wheelchairs, bikes and so on. Paper, paint, felt-tipped pens.

Preparation

Group the wheeled toys together in an area where they are easily accessible to the children and allow them time to play with them. Have the rest of the materials to hand.

What to do

Gather the whole group together and ask them to name some of the equipment in the group that has wheels. Sing the song 'The wheels on the bus' together.

Show them the pictures of things that have wheels and talk about them. Ask the children to name something that they know of that has wheels. It might be something at home, at the shops or something they see outside. Ask them to explain why some things need to have wheels. Some of the children may have bikes. How many wheels do their bikes have? Do they have stabilisers?

Now ask the children to paint a picture of something that has wheels. Help them to count the number of wheels and scribe this for them underneath the painting. For example, 'My lorry has 6 wheels. It has 2 at the front and 4 at the back.' When all the paintings are dry, display them on a wall or screen. Keep the collection of wheeled toys on a table in front of the pictures.

Questions to ask

Are all the wheels different? Why do some things need very big wheels? Do you know anyone who uses a wheelchair? How does it help them? How could you stop a pram or a pushchair rolling away? What happens if you put a brick in front of the wheels?

For younger children

Restrict the activity to play and discussion with very young children.

For older children

Make sets of things with wheels and things without wheels.

Follow-up activities

* Use photocopiable page 94 to reinforce this activity. The children have to find the things with wheels in the picture.
* Make wheeled vehicles with construction toys.
* Make play dough wheels.
* Make a role-play bus with boxes or blocks and seats.
* Make a collection of wheeled toys such as roller skates and toy vehicles.

Links with home

Ask parents/carers to help their child have a go at pushing trolleys or prams. Suggest that they try to spot wheels together on the way to and from the group.

Shoes

Learning outcome

To discover the purposes of a variety of footwear.

Group size

Six to eight children.

What you need

The rhyme 'New shoes' by Ffrida Wolfe on page 77, a collection of footwear including boots, flippers, roller boots and so on. A selection of footwear with different methods of fastening, a large plastic washing basket, several smaller baskets, large sheets of paper, paint, collage materials, felt-tipped pens.

Preparation

Have the rhyme ready and collect the footwear in a large washing basket. Have all the materials to hand.

What to do

Gather the children together in a circle around the basket of shoes. Read the rhyme 'New shoes' to them.

Encourage the children to describe their own pair of shoes. Ask them what colour they are, how they fasten and if they have a pattern on the sole.

Tip the basket of footwear into the middle of the circle and let the children explore them for a short time.

Now ask each child in turn to choose a shoe and say how it is similar or different to his own, when we might wear it and how comfortable or easy it would be to walk in.

When each child has had a turn ask them to paint a picture of their chosen shoes, adding collage materials for decoration.

Display the children's art work with the shoes and the rhyme.

Questions to ask

Who might wear shoes with high heels? What different ways can you think of to fasten your shoes?

For younger children

Reduce the group size to four children. Allow more time for exploration and discussion.

For older children

Encourage the children to sort the shoes into sets using simple criteria such as shoes that buckle, shiny shoes or shoes that tie.

Follow-up activities

✱ Make sole patterns using chalk and black paper.
✱ Make an 'I can tie shoelaces' card.
✱ Make a simple bar chart showing how the children fasten their shoes.
✱ Provide a variety of shoes for the children to use in the role-play area.

Links with home

Ask parents and carers to lend or donate any interesting kinds of footwear they may have, such as ice skates.

Bathtime or bedtime?

Learning outcome

To sort toys to a variety of criteria.

Group size

Four to six children.

What you need

The rhyme 'I had a little brother' (Traditional) on page 78, a selection of toys including fluffy toys, bath toys, dolls, balls and so on, a water tray or baby bath, cot or bed in the role-play area, a large washing basket, a large teddy.

When each child has had a turn, encourage them to put the toy of their choice either in the bed or the bath. Talk about why the choice is successful or not – for example, a fluffy toy in the bath becomes soggy and sinks!

Questions to ask

What will happen if William puts the fluffy duck into the water? Will the boat sink or float in the water? Do you take any toys to bed with you? What are they?

Preparation

Have ready a water tray or baby bath with water in. Make up the cot or bed with a pillow and a blanket and put a large teddy or doll in the bed. Place the collection of toys in a large washing basket.

What to do

Gather the children around the basket of toys in a circle and read the rhyme to them. Show the children the basket of toys and tell them that some of the toys are for Teddy to play with in the bath and some of them are for him to play with in bed. Explain that you would like them to help you sort them into the two sets. Let the children investigate the toys for a short time. Ask each child in turn to choose a toy, describe it and say whether it is suitable for the bath, for bed or for both.

Encourage the others in the group to say whether they agree or disagree and why.

For younger children

Reduce the group size to four and spend time playing with the water toys in the water tray together. Help them to describe the different toys.

For older children

Older children can extend the activity by sorting the toys into different sets and making storage labels for soft toys, water toys, blocks and so on.

Follow-up activities

∗ Set up floating and sinking investigations.
∗ Sort the toys into sets.
∗ Investigate clockwork bath toys.
∗ Find out about materials that soak up water and those that don't.
∗ Set up a display of toys for the bath or for bed.

Links with home

Ask parents or carers to encourage their child to bring in a favourite bath or bed toy for the display.

Sailing away

Learning outcome

To compare the strength of different types of fans.

Group size

Four children.

What you need

Plastic battery-operated fans, folded paper fans, commercially made fans, small plastic or wooden boats, a large water tray, large paper art straws.

Preparation

Have ready the collections of fans, a large water tray filled with water and a selection of small boats.

What to do

Allow the children plenty of time to investigate the fans. Encourage them to discuss how the fans work and how good they are at creating a breeze.

Explain that they are going to race the boats across the water tray. Ask them to choose a boat and a fan. Explain that they must not touch the boats once the race has started. Ask each child in turn to guess which fan will be the best at blowing the boat across the water tray. Can they say why?

After the race, ask each child to report and try to explain what happened with their boat and fan. Ensure that all the children have a turn to race a boat.

Finish by allowing the children to investigate by blowing through art straws to move the boats. What were the similarities and differences between fanning the boat and blowing through the straws?

Questions to ask

Which fan did you think would work best? Were you right? Did it make any difference whether your fan was near or far away from the boat? Can you suggest other uses for fans? How do you keep cool in summer?

For younger children

Allow the younger children more time to play with the fans and boats before the race.

For older children

Encourage the children to race their boats against a minute timer.

Follow-up activities

∗ Make folded and decorated paper fans.
∗ Make a collection of fans.
∗ Make blow patterns by blowing through a straw onto blots of paint on paper.
∗ Make decorated paper windmills.

Links with home

Ask parents to encourage their child to notice and discuss the sounds and effects of wind, as they walk to and from the group.

chapter eight

How things work

In this chapter the children will develop their skills of cutting, folding, joining and building to make a range of products. They will be making decisions about design and which resources and materials they want to use. They will be given opportunities to observe, discuss and use technology.

Make a kite

Learning outcome

To select materials and equipment and develop skills of cutting and joining.

Group size

Four to six children.

What you need

Materials such as sugar paper, tissue paper, shiny paper, thin fabric and plastic sheeting, thin sticks or long pieces of thick card, scissors, adhesive, Sellotape, coloured wool, felt-tipped pens.

Preparation

Collect a variety of simple kites and find some pictures of kites in books.

What to do

Show the children the different kites and look at the pictures in the books. Talk about their shape and the materials that they are made from. Ask the children what they have to do to make a kite work. Take the kites outside and help the children to make them fly.

Now explain that the children can try to make their own kites. Ask them to choose from the different types of paper and material. Suggest that they draw the shape with felt-tipped pens before cutting out the material. They may need some help to cut out some materials, such as plastic. Help them to fix the sticks as a frame or cross-pieces. Let the children decorate their kites with pieces of coloured paper or by drawing with felt-tipped pens. Help them to fix the end of a piece of wool onto their kite and unravel the wool to leave sufficient length for the kite to fly at a low level! Let the children try out their designs.

Questions to ask

What makes the kite work? What is the best type of weather for flying kites? How are you going to make your kite? Which material do you think would be best for a kite? What could you draw or stick onto your kite to make it look attractive?

For younger children

Use different types of paper pre-cut into suitable shapes.

For older children

Encourage older children to add extra features, such as turning their kite into a face or a dragon and add streamers made from tissue or crêpe paper.

Follow-up activities

∗ Ask the children to think of words to describe kites and how they fly. Write these onto cards. Display the kites with the descriptive words.
∗ Read the children poems and stories to do with kites and other things that fly such as *The Blue Balloon* by Mick Inkpen (Hodder).

Links with home

Ask the children to bring in any kites that they have at home.

Lift-the-flap book

Learning outcome

To develop the skills of cutting and sticking.

Group size

Four to six children.

What you need

Sheets of plain paper, pencils, crayons, felt-tipped pens, glue, some lift-the-flap books.

Preparation

Make some blank books about 15cm square using plain paper with four to six pages per book. Collect some published lift-the-flap books such as *Where's Spot?* by Eric Hill (Picture Puffin).

What to do

Read some of the lift-the-flap books to the children. Encourage them to predict what might be under the flap. Use the opportunity to develop the children's positional language, such as behind, under, inside and so on.

Explain to the children how to make their own lift-the-flap books and give them each a blank book. Show them how to make the flaps by drawing and cutting out a picture of an object, such as a toy box, folding an edge and sticking the edge onto the page. They then have to draw a hidden object, such as a ball, behind the flap.

Help them to think of a character for their book and what or who they want to hide behind different features. For example, the book could represent a game of hide-and-seek with pictures of the children and their friends hiding behind things. Be available to help the

children to make the folds and glue down the flap. Allow the children plenty of time to finish their books, it may be necessary to use several sessions. When the books are finished, encourage them to read the books to each other.

Questions to ask

Where would you hide in a game of hide-and-seek? Where can you hide your character? What objects are good to hide behind, or inside, in a house? Where would be a good place to hide outside? What other things could you draw in the picture?

For younger children

Make a lift-the-flap picture with one giant flap.

For older children

Encourage them to do their own writing to go with the pictures or scribe the words for them.

Follow-up activities

* Have blank books available at other times and encourage the children to make different types of books.
* Display a collection of the children's own books in the book area.
* Make some giant-sized books as a group activity.
* Record yourself or one of the children reading these books and let the children use the tape with the books.

Links with home

Ask the children to bring in any lift-the-flap books that they have at home.

Paper bag puppets

Learning outcome

To develop cutting and sticking skills and to select materials to decorate puppets.

Group size

Four to six children.

What you need

Paper bags of different sizes (at least large enough for a child's hand) – strong brown paper ones are the best. A range of material to decorate the puppets – wool, string, coloured paper, fur fabric and so on. Strong glue, scissors.

Preparation

Collect a box of puppets, both manufactured and home-made, in order to develop the children's interest in playing with puppets. Make a sample paper bag puppet to show to the children. Collect some books on making puppets.

What to do

Show the children your paper bag puppet and involve them in a dialogue with the puppet. Explain how you made the puppet and why you decided to use the materials that you selected.

Show the children the materials that you have collected and the different sizes of paper bag. Ask them to think of a puppet that they would like to make. It might be an animal, a clown or a character from a story. Talk to each child about what materials they will need to make their puppet. Let them select their resources and work on their own design. They may need some help with cutting and sticking difficult materials. Help the children to think about where they want to position the features on their paper bag. When they have finished their puppets, let them make up a puppet show with their friends.

Questions to ask

Will your puppet be an animal or a person? What type of hair will your puppet need? What shape will the ears be? What will it need on its face? Will the mouth be happy, sad or something else? What is your puppet's name?

For younger children

Limit the choice of materials and make sure that they are easy to cut.

For older children

Ask them to work in pairs or a small group to make up a story using their puppet characters.

Follow-up activities

∗ Develop the theme to make different types of puppets, such as rod puppets and finger puppets.
∗ Make a puppet theatre by draping material over a clothes horse or cutting out the front of a big cardboard box.
∗ Ask the children to make a puppet theatre out of big blocks or other construction materials.

Links with home

Let the children take the puppets home with a photocopied sheet showing how puppets can be made from simple things such as paper bags.

Design a hat

Learning outcome

To develop cutting and sticking skills and to select materials to decorate the hat.

Group size
Four to six children.

What you need

Strips of card 4cm wide and long enough to go round a child's head. Circles cut from thin card ready to fold into a cone shape. Scissors, adhesive and a range of materials such as shiny paper, sequins, coloured shapes, old greetings cards, plain card, felt-tipped pens and crayons to decorate the hat. A stapler for joining the card.

Preparation

A collection of party hats made from card. Try to organise this activity for a time when the children will be having a party. Make a band hat and a cone hat to show to the children.

What to do

Look at the party hats with the children and let them pass them on. Ask them which ones they like best and why.

Show the children the hats that you have made and explain how you have to measure the band, or fold the cone shape, to fit the size of a child's head. Ask the children to choose which type of hat they would like to make. Fold the card to fit their heads and help them to staple it in place. Now let them choose what materials they want to use to decorate their hat. Help them to cut out difficult shapes and to use the glue carefully. Make sure that the children have an opportunity to use their hats, preferably during a party.

Questions to ask

What type of hat are you going to make? What are you going to choose to put on your hat? What pictures or patterns could you draw or stick on your hat? What clothes would go with your hat? When might you wear a hat?

For younger children

Concentrate on making just the band type hats, and have some bands ready made for them to select one that fits.

For older children

Ask them to design a 'character' hat, such as a pirate or a king or queen.

Follow-up activities

✳ Make a collection of exotic hats for use in role-play. Keep these in a special box or treasure trove with other decorative items such as jewellery, old keys and little treasures.

✳ Develop the theme to include masks and show the children how to make simple card masks.

Links with home

Invite parents in to help with the hat making and the party.

Build a house

Learning outcome

To develop skills of designing and making.

Group size
Four to six children.

What you need
A selection of cereal boxes, pieces of card, old newspapers, paper, scissors, paste to make glue, pots with spreaders, pencils, paints, paintbrushes, pictures of houses.

Preparation
Mix up dried paste with water. Encourage the children to notice the change that takes place when water is added. Cover a table with newspaper and put the tools and materials on it.

What to do
Show the children the pictures of houses. Talk about the similarities and differences between their homes and the houses in the pictures.

Explain that they are going to make a house. Discuss the features that they will need to include such as windows, doors, and so on. Let the children choose a box to make their house.

Help the children to choose the correct size of paper to cover each face of the box. Show them how to do this by putting the box on the paper, drawing round the outline and cutting out. Next, encourage the children to experiment with pasting paper onto their box. Notice what happens if too much or not enough glue is applied. Do they need to cover all the paper with glue? Which parts are the most important to cover?

Discuss the different ways of making doors and windows – cutting shapes out of the box or sticking on pieces of card to make flaps where the windows and doors will be. Refer to the pictures from time to time. Which other features could they add?

Paint the houses and when dry add detail with felt-tipped pens. On a large piece of paper, paint a road. Display the houses by sticking them onto the paper, lined up along the road. Build up the picture over a period of time by adding trees, flowers and people.

Questions to ask
How can we measure the paper to fit the side of the box? What might we use to make a roof? Why is the box more difficult to cut than the paper?

For younger children
Spend time beforehand developing sticking skills.

For older children
Ask older children to design their house by drawing or painting it before they make it.

Follow-up activities
* Go for a walk along a street nearby to look at the houses.
* Build houses using construction materials.
* Make some other buildings, such as a shop or a church, with groups of children.

Links with home
Ask parents or carers to do a 'walkabout' at home with their child, counting rooms, stairs, windows and so on.

Baking buns

Learning outcome

To observe the changes that take place when cake mixture is cooked and to use technology.

Group size

Four to six children.

What you need

The rhyme 'Five currant buns' on page 87. The ingredients: 450g plain flour, 50g butter, 1 egg, 1 level tsp salt, 50g castor sugar, 1 level tsp dried yeast, 150ml lukewarm milk, 4 tablespoons lukewarm water, 125g currants. Utensils: bowls, hand whisk, tablespoon, teaspoon, jug, weighing scales, tea towel, kneading board, baking tray, oven, oven gloves, mechanical timer, washing-up equipment. Aprons.

Preparation

Sing the rhyme 'Five currant buns' together. Explain that they are going to make some buns to use as they say the rhyme. Have ready the ingredients and utensils on a table. Ensure the children wash their hands and put on an apron.

What to do

Show the children each ingredient in turn and explain what you are doing as you set the oven temperature. Warn them that ovens get very hot and they should not touch them or go near them.

Allow the children to take part at each stage of making the buns. Sift 100g of flour into a bowl, adding a teaspoon of sugar. Blend the yeast with milk and water and add to the bowl. Mix well and leave until frothy (about 20 minutes). Meanwhile mix the rest of the flour, sugar, salt and currants in

a separate bowl and add to the yeast mixture with beaten egg and butter. Knead on a board for five minutes. Cover and leave it to rise to double its size. Now knead the mixture lightly and divide into 12 equal pieces, shape the pieces into buns and place on a prepared baking tray.

Cover and leave to rise for about 30 minutes. Ask the children to describe what the mixture is like, to say how it has changed and predict how it might change when it is cooked. Bake in the centre of an oven (425°F/220°C/gas mark 7) for about 20 minutes.

When the buns are cooked allow them to cool before letting the children handle them. Discuss the changes that have taken place. Play a game with the rhyme using the real buns.

Questions to ask

How has the mixture changed? How would we make the buns into a different shape? What would happen if we left the buns in a hot oven all night?

For younger children

Work in small groups of three to four children.

For older children

Write and illustrate a recipé for making buns.

Follow-up activities

* Equip a role-play area with baking equipment, an oven and a timer.
* Make some mini Christmas cakes in small clean baked bean tins with masking tape covering sharp edges.
* Design 'special' buns, such as buns with faces using icing, Smarties and so on.

Links with home

Before the activity ensure that parents/carers have been asked if there are any foods that their child must not eat due to allergies, religious or cultural reasons. Ensure that you use a recipe that everyone in the group can eat.

Popping corn

Learning outcome

To observe the changes that take place to popcorn when it is cooked.

Group size

Six children.

What you need

A microwave oven, packets of microwave popping corn (available from most large supermarkets), plastic bowls, spoons.

Preparation

Read the instructions on the popcorn packet carefully beforehand. Have ready a microwave oven and any bowls or materials required to pop the corn.

What to do

Gather the children round the table. Open a packet of uncooked popcorn and give each child a spoonful to investigate. Warn them not to put the small pieces in their mouths. Ask them to describe how it feels, looks and what they think it might be. Does it remind them of any other food? Ask the children if they have had popcorn before, perhaps at the cinema. Did it look like this? Explain that you are going to cook the kernels in the microwave to change it into edible popcorn.

Encourage the children to predict what changes will take place when the corn is cooked. Cook the corn following the instructions on the packet. Show the children which buttons you will be pressing to time the cooking and start the machine. Listen to the corn cooking. Can the children explain the noises they hear?

When the corn is cooked, give a small amount to each child and discuss with them the changes that have taken place. Encourage them to touch, smell and taste the popcorn.

Questions to ask

Do any of the children have microwaves at home? How else do people cook food? Which foods can we eat without cooking? Which foods have to be cooked?

For younger children

Concentrate on developing the vocabulary to describe shape, size, colour and feel of the corn cooked and uncooked. Make sure they do not put the uncooked kernels in their mouths.

For older children

Make 'before' and 'after' pictures illustrating the changes that took place.

Follow-up activities

* Cut out pictures from magazines and catalogues to make a chart of different kinds of cookers.
* Make kitchen safety posters.
* Make a microwave and conventional cooker out of boxes, paper, paint, felt-tipped pens and collage materials.

Links with home

Ask parents or carers to provide opportunities for their child to see and discuss the changes that take place when food is cooked.

Sing a song of sixpence

Learning outcome

To use technology (a cassette recorder) for an appropriate purpose.

Group size

Four to six children.

What you need

A collection of nursery rhymes and songs, tape-recorder or listening centre, 30 minute blank tape, pre-recorded nursery rhyme or song tape, a quiet area.

Preparation

Over a planned period, focus the whole group on favourite nursery rhymes and songs, encouraging the children to develop their repertoire of known rhymes/songs.

Set up a listening area with a tape-recorder, headphones and pre-recorded nursery rhyme tape.

What to do

Work in a quiet area. Explain that you would like to work with the children to make a rhyme tape for a birthday party. Ask them to suggest some favourite rhymes/songs and help the group to choose one of them. Show them how the tape fits into the machine and explain the function of the buttons, showing them which must be pressed to record. Use coloured stickers to help children remember which buttons to press.

Ask the children to start singing the chosen rhyme for you to record. Begin recording them as they sing or say the rhyme. Replay the tape and then repeat the process until a tape has been produced featuring several rhymes/songs. Use as a resource in the listening corner.

Questions to ask

Which is your favourite rhyme? How will we know which buttons to press? Where else can we listen to songs, stories and rhymes? How can we share our rhyme with other children?

For younger children

Select three or four known rhymes from which the children can choose. Carry out the activity with a group of three or four children.

For older children

Make a collection of rhyme cards or a booklet to accompany the tape. Make written or pictorial instructions for how to use a tape-recorder.

Follow-up activities

* Make a collection of nursery rhymes, poetry and song anthologies.
* Make a rhyme book including poems made by the children.
* Compile a group tape of counting rhymes.
* Ask children to record their own stories.
* Create a role-play area such as Humpty Dumpty's wall.
* Make miniature 'Mary Mary' gardens in seed trays.

Links with home

Invite parents or carers to listen to the tape that the children have made. Copy the tape several times as a resource for the children to borrow.

Greetings!

Learning outcome

To develop skills of folding and measuring.

Group size

Four to six children.

What you need

A selection of greeting cards, thin card of different sizes, sheets of paper, collage materials such as tissue paper, sticky paper and sequins. Pencils, felt-tipped pens, glue, glue pots, paste spreaders, crayons.

Preparation

Choose an appropriate time such as Christmas, Mother's Day, Divali, Chinese New Year or Eid. Explain that many people send cards to each other on special occasions. Talk about times when they have received cards. Ensure that all the materials are accessible to the group.

What to do

Gather the children together and show them the selection of cards. Encourage them to notice the common features of cards and ways in which they are different. Notice how the cards are folded, where they are decorated and where there is a message.

Ask the children to choose one person, perhaps a member of their family, to whom they would like to send a card. Allow them to fold their own pieces of paper or card. Ask them to say where the decoration and writing will be. Make the cards using collage materials and/or pictures and patterns with colouring materials. When the cards are finished let each child write their own message.

Show the children the envelopes and provide time for them to investigate cutting, folding and sticking pieces of paper to make envelopes.

Questions to ask

What could you use to make a flower for the card? What do you notice about the edges of these cards when they are folded over? Which is easier to fold, the paper or the card? How will we make sure that the card fits inside the envelope?

For younger children

Provide opportunities for children to develop cutting, sticking and folding skills, before the activity. Be available to help them throughout the activity.

For older children

Encourage the children to write their own message. Suggest that they try experimenting with different ways of folding their cards, such as zigzag cards.

Follow-up activities

* Make a huge group card for a special occasion.
* Set up a card shop with materials available to make and 'sell' cards.
* Design and make gift wrapping paper.
* Wrap up boxes to make parcels.

Links with home

Ask the children's families to help them make a card at home for someone special. Ask them to show their child any special cards that they have kept, such as 'New Baby' cards to celebrate the child's birth.

Magnet car game

Learning outcome

To select materials and equipment for a task and to develop cutting, folding and joining skills.

Group size
Four to six children.

What you need
Roadway playmat. Sheets of white A3 card, smaller pieces of thin white card (approximately 8cm square), some strips of card 6cm × 2cm, glue, paint, crayons and felt-tipped pens, paper-clips and some magnets. Photocopiable page 95.

Preparation
Make a small car out of card and glue onto a folded strip of card as shown in the diagram. Fix a paper-clip to the base. Make copies of the photocopiable sheet onto card ready for the children to use.

What to do
Place the car onto a larger piece of card and move the magnet around under it. This should make the car move around on the surface. Explain to the children that the car needs a road to move along. Show the children the roadway on the playmat and ask the children to make their own roadway on an A3 piece of card.

Ask them to select materials to colour this in and to draw other features such as houses, trees and traffic lights.

Now invite them to make their own cars or vehicles using the photocopiable sheet. Help the children to fold the card in half and to fix the paper-clip onto the base. Let them use their magnets to make the cars move along their roadway.

Questions to ask
What makes the cars move? Can they make their cars stay on the road? What other vehicles could they make for their game? What features could they draw or stick onto their board? What markings might you see on the road? What other materials are attracted to a magnet?

For younger children
Fold the pieces of card for them.

For older children
Ask them to use the folded card technique to stick some objects onto their roadway such as trees and houses. These would then form real obstacles for their cars to move in between.

Follow-up activities
∗ Talk to the children about road safety and where they should cross the road.

∗ Practise crossing the road using a chalk road marked outside, or a road made from paper or a sheet inside. Talk to the children about the best places to cross a road.

∗ Take small groups of children to walk around the neighbourhood. Draw their attention to some of the features near the roads such as shops, houses and grassy areas. Talk about the safest places to cross the road.

∗ Let the children investigate which materials are attracted to magnets.

Links with home

Ask the children to think about any car games that they have at home. Let them borrow the magnets to find out what materials are attracted to magnets at home.

Name _____

Child records

Knowledge and Understanding of the World		Assessment and comments	
Skills and concepts	**Baseline/1st assessment Date**	**2nd assessment Date**	**End of year assessment Date**
SCIENCE			
Can explore and recognise features of: ✱ objects and events in the natural and made world; ✱ living things.			
Looks closely at: ✱ similarites; ✱ differences; ✱ patterns; ✱ change.			
Asks questions about: ✱ why things happen; ✱ how things work.			
Can: ✱ talk about his/her observations. ✱ record his/her observations.			

Child records

Name _____

Knowledge and Understanding of the World		Assessment and comments	
Skills and concepts	**Baseline/1st assessment Date**	**2nd assessment Date**	**End of year assessment Date**
HISTORY			
Can talk about: ✱ own family;			
✱ past and present;			
✱ events in own life.			
GEOGRAPHY			
Can talk about: ✱ where he/she lives;			
✱ own environment;			
✱ some features of the area.			

Name _____

Child records

Knowledge and Understanding of the World		Assessment and comments	
Skills and concepts	Baseline/1st assessment Date	2nd assessment Date	End of year assessment Date
DESIGN AND TECHNOLOGY			
Can: ✻ explore and select materials and equipment.			
Uses the skills of: ✻ cutting; ✻ folding; ✻ joining; ✻ building.			
INFORMATION TECHNOLOGY			
Can: ✻ Use technology as appropriate (note which type, for example, tape-recorder, calculator, telephone, computer and so on).			

Laura

Baby Laura's the youngest in our house.
There's her sister called Naomi
she calls her
Maymee.
There's her mum
who she calls
Mum.
There's me
she calls Daddo, (though I'm not her real dad)
and there's my two boys, Joe and Eddie
who live with me for half the week
and live with their mum for the other half of the week.
Laura calls
Joe,
Doe
and she calls Eddie,
Deddie.
So there you have it
Mum, Daddo, Maymee, Doe and Deddie.

At bedtime she has to kiss us all good night.
Ny ny, she says
Ny ny
and she pushes out her lips
to make a kiss
and round she goes,
Maymee, Doe, Deddie, Daddo and Mum,
though sometimes she jumps into Joe's bed
and pretends she's asleep in there.
Yesterday she stuffed a little plastic camel
in the place where the tapes go in the video.
So the video doesn't work anymore.
Maybe she thought that if you put a plastic camel in there
the machine will copy it and
more plastic camels will come out.
The other day she got into the shopping
and starting crunching up the Weetabix all over the floor
and then mixing it with the eggs.
Maybe she thought that she was cooking Weetabix omelettes.
You can never tell what she's thinking.

Michael Rosen

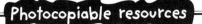
Weather Bear

Weather Bear,
Weather Bear,
Looks at the weather
Then decides what to wear.

It's hot today.
My T-shirt and shorts
Will keep me cool.
Then I'll put on my trunks
And jump in the pool.

It's windy today.
I'll put on my anorak
When I go out
And tie my scarf tight
So it won't blow about.
It's raining today.
I'll wear my wellies
And my waterproof mac.
My umbrella will keep
The rain off my back.

It's cold today.
I'll put on a sweater
And a warm winter coat,
Thick gloves on my paws
And a scarf round my throat.

Weather Bear,
Weather Bear,
Looks at the weather
Then decides what to wear.

John Foster

New shoes

New shoes, new shoes,
Red and pink and blue shoes,
Tell me what would *you* choose
If they'd let us buy?

Buckle shoes, bow shoes,
Pretty pointy-toe shoes,
Strappy, cappy low shoes;
Let's have some to try.

Bright shoes, white shoes,
Dandy dance-by-night shoes,
Perhaps a-little-tight shoes;
Like some? So would I.

BUT

Flat shoes, fat shoes,
Stump-along-like-that shoes,
Wipe-them-on-the-mat shoes
O that's the sort they'll buy.

Ffrida Wolfe

Five little peas

Five little peas in a pea-pod pressed,
One grew, two grew and so did all the rest.
They grew and grew and did not stop,
Until one day the pod
Went
POP!

Traditional

I had a little brother

I had a little brother
His name was Tiny Tim,
I put him in the bath tub
To teach him how to swim.

He drank up all the water,
He ate up all the soap,
He was sick last night
With a bubble in his throat.

In came the doctor,
In came the nurse,
In came the lady
With the alligator purse.

'He's sick,' said the doctor,
'He's sick,' said the nurse.
'He's sick,' said the lady
With the alligator purse.

Out went the doctor,
Out went the nurse,
Out went the lady
With the alligator purse.

Traditional

A present for Granny

'Has anyone got a good idea for Granny's birthday present?' asked Mum at breakfast one morning.

'Flowers,' said Dad. 'She loves them.'

'But she's always got lots in the garden at this time of year,' Mum replied.

'A vase for her flowers then,' suggested Ben.

'Difficult to send in the post,' said Dad.

'I know,' said Lizzie. Everyone looked at her. Lizzie was four and the youngest in the family. 'A photo of us all together. Granny's always saying she wishes she could see more of us.'

'What a good idea!' said Mum. 'Auntie Jenny, Uncle Bill and the twins could be in it too. I'll try to fix it for Saturday.' And she did.

Mrs Hunter, the photographer, arrived early on Saturday morning and set up her special lights in the sitting room. Then Uncle Bill, Auntie Jenny and the twins arrived. Ben and Lizzie took their cousins in to Mrs Hunter. She sat all the children on the sofa. They had to move the cat. Ben put her on his lap. The grown-ups stood behind.

'Get ready with a great big smile,' said Mrs Hunter. Everyone smiled. Except Lizzie.

'Pop should be in the picture,' she said. Pop was the goldfish.

'Fine,' said Mrs Hunter. She and Dad lifted the tank carefully onto the coffee table.

'Everyone ready?' she asked. They all nodded. Except Lizzie.

'I want Hugs in the photo,' she said. Hugs was her favourite teddy.

'Would you like to fetch him?' sighed Mrs Hunter.

It took fifteen minutes to find Hugs. Everyone had to help Lizzie hunt for him. At last Auntie Jenny found him under a cushion in one of the armchairs.

'Right. Here we go,' said Mum, trying to sound calm.

They hurried back to their places.

Everyone began to smile. Except Lizzie. A big tear trickled down her cheek.

'Oh dear,' said Mrs Hunter.

'What's the matter?' asked Dad.

'Granny will be sad if Ruff isn't in the photo. She loves him.'

Everyone looked round. No one had seen Ruff all morning. They shouted his name. They waited. There was a pattering sound in the hall. Ruff dashed in with a bone in his mouth. He had dirt on his nose and his fur was very messy.

'Stop him!' said Mum.

But it was too late. Ruff jumped onto Lizzie's lap and snuggled down. He wagged his tail. Lizzie smiled. Everyone else laughed. Mrs Hunter pressed the button on her camera.

'Got it! At last!' she said.

'Granny will be pleased,' said Lizzie. And Granny was.

Jillian Harker

 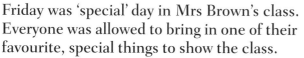

Something special

Friday was 'special' day in Mrs Brown's class. Everyone was allowed to bring in one of their favourite, special things to show the class.

'What can I take that's special?' asked Charlie one Friday morning.

Mum was busy feeding Sally. 'What about your teddy?' she said.

'Lots of people take their teddies,' said Charlie. 'I want to take something different.'

Sally started crying.

'Look in your bedroom,' said Mum.

Charlie searched through his things. There was Bessie, the old rag doll from Africa that had belonged to his grandma. But she didn't look very special with her stuffing coming out.

There was the model boat he'd made all by himself. But it fell apart as soon as he tried to pick it up.

There was the beautiful chocolate rabbit he'd saved from Easter. But one ear had been bitten off.

'I can't find anything,' said Charlie sadly. 'Can you help me look?'

Mum was busy dressing Sally.

'There's no time now,' she said. 'Don't look so miserable. We can find something for next week.'

When they got to school the other children had lots of special things.

Raju had some sweet and sticky gulab jamun that smelt of rose petals, and he let everyone taste them.

Peter had a strange looking plant called a 'Venus Fly Trap'. He said it ate flies and would eat your finger if you weren't careful.

Lu Mei had a beautiful kite. It was made of bright red paper and shaped like a dragon. She said it came from China.

Charlie's best friend Steven brought in his pet hamster in a cage. Steven said its name was Biscuit and Joanne said it looked like a rat.

And Daniel had a huge slimy worm that he'd found on the way to school, but Mrs Brown made him put it outside.

Shireen had a beautiful sari that sparkled blue and gold. She put it on and Mrs Brown said she looked like a princess.

But Charlie had nothing.

'Never mind,' said Mrs Brown. 'You can bring something to show us next week.'

'But I haven't got anything special,' said Charlie on his way home. 'Not special and different.'

'What about your favourite book? Or Goldie the fish? Or your collection of postcards from Uncle Ali in Nigeria?'

Mum tried hard to think of something.

'No, I don't want to take those,' said Charlie.

When they got home Mum had to feed Sally again. And change her nappy. And wash her clothes. And put her to bed.

Charlie felt cross. He turned the television on really loud. He stamped around and slammed the door.

'Ssh! You'll wake your sister,' said Mum.

'I don't care!' said Charlie to himself.

Charlie felt Mum would never have time to help him find something special.

On Saturday they had to go to the shops in the rain, because Mum had to buy more nappies for Sally.

On Sunday Auntie Jill and Uncle John came, and they made a big fuss of Sally all day.

On Monday they were late for school because Sally had cried all night and they slept in.

On Tuesday Charlie went to Steven's house for tea. Steven had lots of special things. 'You can borrow something if you like,' he said.

'But it wouldn't be mine,' said Charlie.

On Wednesday Charlie felt very cross. He still couldn't think of anything special to take to school. And Sally was crying again.

Mum was busy making biscuits in the kitchen.

'You go to her,' she said.

'I don't want to.' Charlie stamped his foot and started to cry. 'All she does is cry all the time and I haven't got anything that's special, nothing at all.'

Mum took Charlie onto her knee. 'We'll find you something, you'll see. Now you go up and see Sally for me while I get the biscuits finished. Then you can have some warm from the oven, just how you like them.'

Charlie went slowly up the stairs and into Sally's room. He covered his ears and looked at his sister. Her face was all screwed up like an angry prune and she was kicking her legs wildly in the air.

'Stupid babies,' he muttered. He picked up one of Sally's baby toys and started to play with it.

Sally stopped screaming. Charlie looked into the cot. Sally looked at Charlie with her big brown eyes. Charlie looked at Sally. Her hands were so tiny!

He reached out and touched her fingers. She grabbed on to his finger so tightly he nearly cried out. But it felt nice. He didn't know babies were so strong.

'Hello, Sally,' he said. And then Sally did something she'd never done before. She smiled. A big beaming smile, just for Charlie.

Later that evening Mum came to tuck Charlie into bed. She held a wonderful carved wooden mask. 'I've found something for you to take to school,' she said.

'But I've already got something,' said Charlie, and whispered in Mum's ear.

At school on Thursday Charlie was very excited. 'I'm bringing something really special tomorrow,' he said.

'Is it a new toy?' asked Lu Mei.

'No,' said Charlie.

'Is it your goldfish?' asked Steven.

'No,' said Charlie.

'Is it something you can eat?' asked Daniel.

'No,' said Charlie. 'I'm not telling.'

At last it was Friday. The other children were already waiting when Mum brought Charlie into the classroom.

'Charlie has something special to show us this morning,' said Mrs Brown.

'This is my baby sister,' said Charlie proudly. 'She's called Sally and she's six weeks old and she smiles at me and she's very, very special.'

'She looks like you,' said Peter.

'When will she be big enough to play football?' said Daniel.

'You are lucky,' said Joanne.

'I wish I had a baby sister,' said Lu Mei.

'She isn't smiling at me,' said Steven.

'She only smiles at me,' said Charlie, 'because I'm her brother.'

That night Charlie helped Mum to bath Sally and put her to bed.

'Do you know what special day it will be tomorrow?' asked Mum, when Sally was asleep.

'No,' said Charlie.

'It's going to be 'big brother day', said Mum. 'A special day for big brothers, because big brothers really are 'something special'.'

Nicola Moon

A visit to the park

'Here's the park, Grandpa,' said Sarah. 'Now I'll show you my favourite place.'

She grabbed her grandfather's hand, and pulled him towards the playground.

'Wait for us!' yelled her brother Mark, as he hurried after them with his dad and his friend, Paul.

In the playground Sarah ran straight to the monkey bars. She jumped up and swung across them calling, 'Look at me, Grandpa!'

She dropped down and made for the climbing frame. Mark and Paul were already there. Paul stood on the wobbly bridge and shook it as Sarah crossed over. They both laughed. Mark peered at her through the big plastic window that made your face look really huge.

'Yuk!' said Sarah. 'A giant Mark.'

They headed for the slide and zoomed down, kicking up sand as they landed at the bottom.

'Come on, Grandpa,' called Sarah, as she, Mark and Paul swayed to and fro on seats fixed to a huge spring. 'There's room for you too.'

'Now I want to show Grandpa my favourite place,' said Mark, jumping off. 'I want him to see the pond.'

Mark led his grandfather to the edge of the pond. In the middle lay a small island where a group of ducks sat, preening their feathers.

'Look!' whispered Mark, and pointed at a large dragonfly as it whizzed round over the pond.

'In the spring there are frogs everywhere,'

Mark told his grandfather. 'Aren't there Dad?' Dad nodded.

Mark picked up a small twig and placed it carefully on the water.

'Bet I can get it between those lily leaves,' he said, and blew hard behind it. The twig floated over the pond and bumped into one of the leaves.

'Better luck next time,' said his grandfather.

'What about you Paul?' Grandfather asked. 'Where's your favourite place in the park?'

'I like the corner over by the picnic tables,' said Paul. 'I'll show you.'

'Good idea,' said Dad. 'I just happen to have some apples and drinks in my bag.'

As they munched their apples, Paul explained how the park-keepers changed the flower-beds through the year.

'There's always something new to look at. There are tons of butterflies now,' he said, pointing. 'In autumn I just like to crunch through all the leaves from these trees.'

'What's your favourite bit, Grandpa?' asked Sarah.

'Well,' said Grandpa. 'The playground's very exciting. I thought the pond was really interesting. And here, it's so peaceful. I think...'

The three children waited.

'I like it all,' he finished.

'Thank goodness!' smiled Dad. 'That keeps everyone happy.'

Jillian Harker

I've got a body

And on that body
I've got some hands
And they go everywhere with me.
And I clap clap here,
Clap clap there,
Clap clap clap clap everywhere.
Sniff sniff here,
Sniff sniff there,
Sniff sniff sniff sniff everywhere.
I've got a body...

And on that body
I've got some feet
And they go everywhere with me.
And I stamp stamp here,
Stamp stamp there,
Stamp stamp stamp stamp everywhere.
Clap clap here...
Sniff sniff here...
I've got a body...

Harriet Powell

The bear went over the mountain

Traditional

The wheels on the bus

Joyfully

The wheels on the bus go round and round,
Round and round, Round and round. The wheels on the bus go round and round,
All day long. long.

The people on the bus go up and down
Up and down, up and down.
The people on the bus go up and down
All day long.

The children on the bus have fun fun fun
Fun fun fun, fun fun fun
The children on the bus have fun fun fun
All day long.

Arranged by Johanne Levy

Birthday song

With a swing

1.It's some-one's birth-day to-day, Hap-py birth-day to

you! You've got a lit-tle bit old-er And a lit-tle bit tal-ler too. *Chorus* So

stand up where we can see you, There's some-thing we want to say, We'll

all join to-geth-er to wish you Ve-ry ma-ny hap-py re-turns of the day!

It's someone's birthday today,
Happy birthday to you!
You've got a little bit older
And a little bit taller, too.

Chorus

So stand up where we can see you,
There's something we want to say,
We'll all join together to wish you
Very many happy returns of the day!

So light the candles and blow
Happy birthday to you!
You've got a little bit older
You can blow a bit harder, too!

Chorus

Jan Holdstock

Five currant buns

Choose a different child each time until all the children have had a turn.

Four currant buns...
Three currant buns...
Two...
One...

Arranged by Johanne Levy

For baby and me

Draw some toys for the baby and some toys for you.

Toys for a baby.

Toys for me.

The new baby (P23)

Family wedding

Family photo (p27)

Dotty ladybirds

Give each ladybird eight dots.

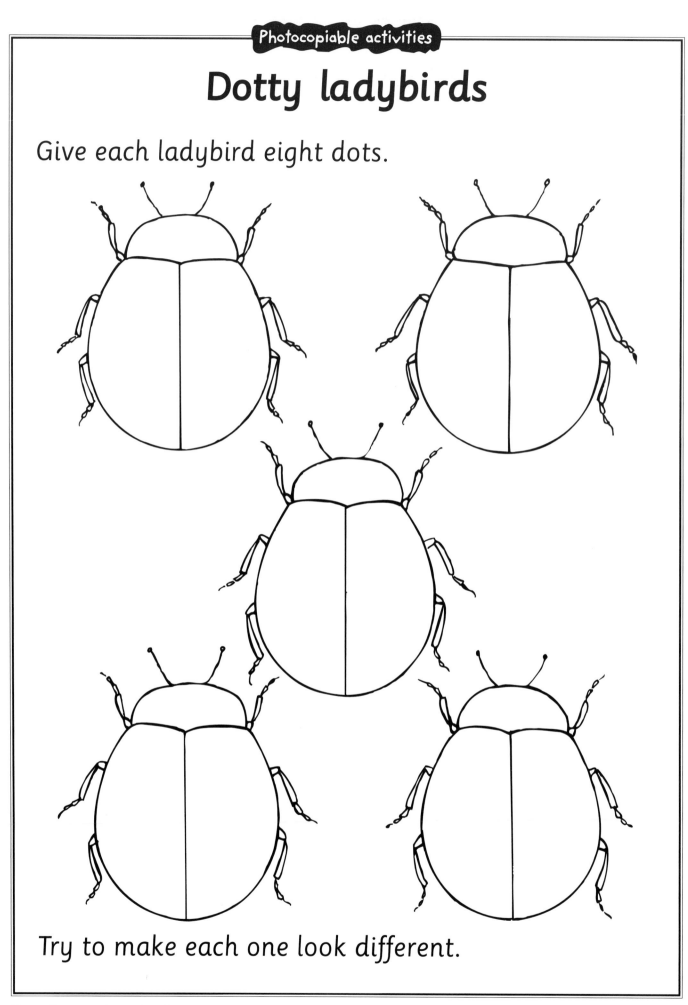

Try to make each one look different.

Home for a minibeast (p34)

Where's mummy?

Help me find my mummy. Draw her in the box.

Where's my mummy? (p35)

Who lives here?

Draw an animal to live in each home.

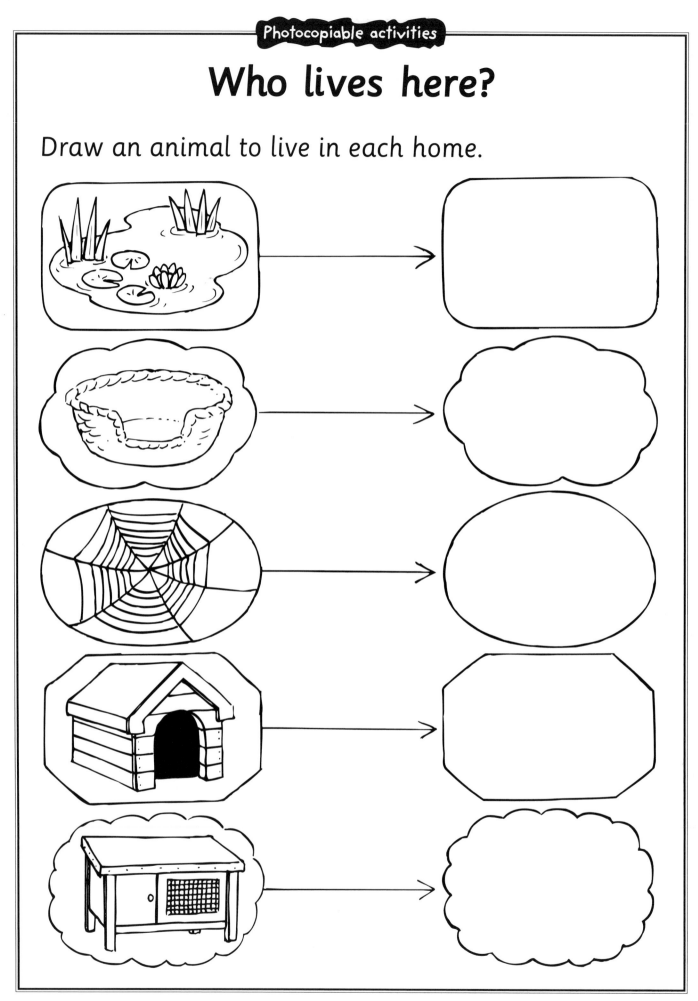

Who lives here? (p36)

Weather chart

Look at the weather each day and draw what the weather is like below.

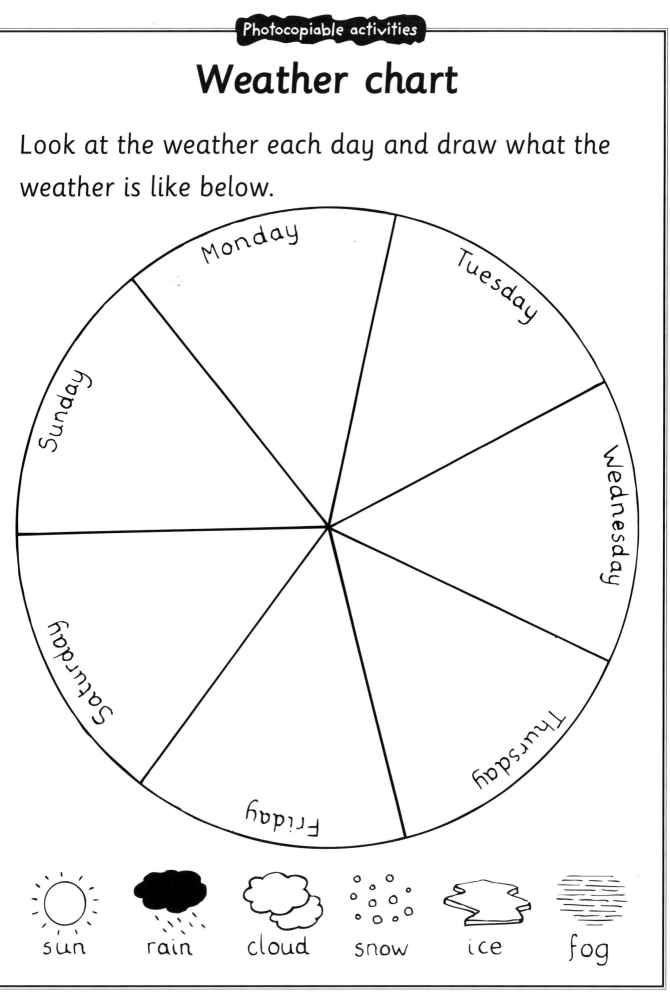

Weather bear (p44)

Find the wheels

Find the things with wheels in the picture.

Draw a circle around the wheels and colour the picture.

Fun with wheels (p59)

Cut out cars

Cut out the vehicles and glue them onto folded
pieces of card.

Magnet car game (p72)

Resources

Teacher reference books

Themes for early years – Weather Linda Mort and Janet Morris (Scholastic)

Learning through play – Small world play Barbara J Leach, *The home corner* Su Garnett (Scholastic)

Studies in Early Years 7: Science (SES Publications) Shropshire Education Services, The Shire Hall, Shrewsbury, Shropshire SY2 6ND

Story books

Avocado Baby John Burningham (Red Fox)

My Great Grandpa Martin Waddell (Walker)

When Grandma Came Jill Paton Walsh and Sophy Williams (Picture Puffin)

All Join In Quentin Blake (Red Fox)

Rosie Plants a Radish Kate Petty and Alex Scheffler (Macmillan)

It's My Birthday Helen Oxenbury (Walker)

Mrs Wobble the Waitress Janet and Allan Ahlberg (Young Puffin)

Mrs Vole the Vet Allan Ahlberg and Emma Chichester-Clark *Happy Families Series* (Puffin)

Spot's Birthday Party, Spot's Baby Sister Eric Hill (Picture Puffin)

Information books

How Does Your Garden Grow? Kate Burns and Dawn Apperley (Levinson Books)

The Tiny Seed Eric Carle (Picture Puffin)

The World is Full of Babies Mick Manning/Brita Granstrom (Watts Books)

Let's Look at Growing Nicola Tuxworth (Lorenz Books)

Whose Home? David Bennett and Julie Lacombe *Parent and Child Series* (Picture Mammoth)

Song, poetry and rhyme books

The Helen Oxenbury Nursery Rhyme Book (Heinemann)

All Together Now Nick Butterworth (Picture Lions)

The Wheels on the Bus Paul Zelinsky (Orchard Books)

Games and puzzles

Things In My House – picture-matching game (Ravensburger).

NES Arnold jigsaw puzzles: Children of the world, Celebration jigsaws, Family outings jigsaws, 'Our children' jigsaws.

Galt jigsaws: Double-sided farmyard puzzle, High Street playboard, Scenic puzzles pack, Talkabout puzzle – playground.

Equipment

Multicultural dolls, dressing-up clothes (NES Arnold).

Farmyard builder – a construction game (Ravensburger), available from NES Arnold.

Play shop/food, play farm, farm set and farm animals. Tool kit, magnifier and prism scope, giant magnet, minibeast viewer (Early Learning Centre).

Construction, sand, water, role-play and small world resources available from NES Arnold, Hope Education and Galt.

Useful addresses

Association of Science Education, College Lane, Hatfield, Hertfordshire AL10 9AA. Tel: 01707 267411.

British Association for Early Childhood Education (BAECE), 111 City View House, 463 Bethnal Green Road London, E2 9QY. Tel: 0171 739 7594.

Pre-school Learning Alliance, 69 Kings Cross Road, London WC1X 9LL. Tel: 0171 833 0991.

NES Arnold Ltd, Ludlow Hill Road, West Bridgford, Nottingham, NG2 6HD.

Hope Education, Orb Mill, Huddersfield Road, Waterhead, Oldham, Lancashire OL4 2ST.

Early Learning Centre, South Marston Park, Swindon, SN3 4TJ.